Jama Masjid

Call of the Soul

NL Batra

Foreword by Professor Mushirul Hasan

Published by
NIYOGI BOOKS
Block D, Building No. 77,
Okhla Industrial Area, Phase-I,
New Delhi-110 020, INDIA
Tel: 91-11-26816301, 26818960
Email: niyogibooks@gmail.com
Website: www.niyogibooksindia.com

ISBN: 978-93-86906-53-3
Publication: 2006
First paperback edition: 2018

Photographs: Archaeological Survey of India, DN Choudhury,
DN Dubey, Plaza Colour Lab & Studio, Asia Photo Studio, VK Maini

Printed at: Niyogi Offset Pvt. Ltd., New Delhi, India

Contents

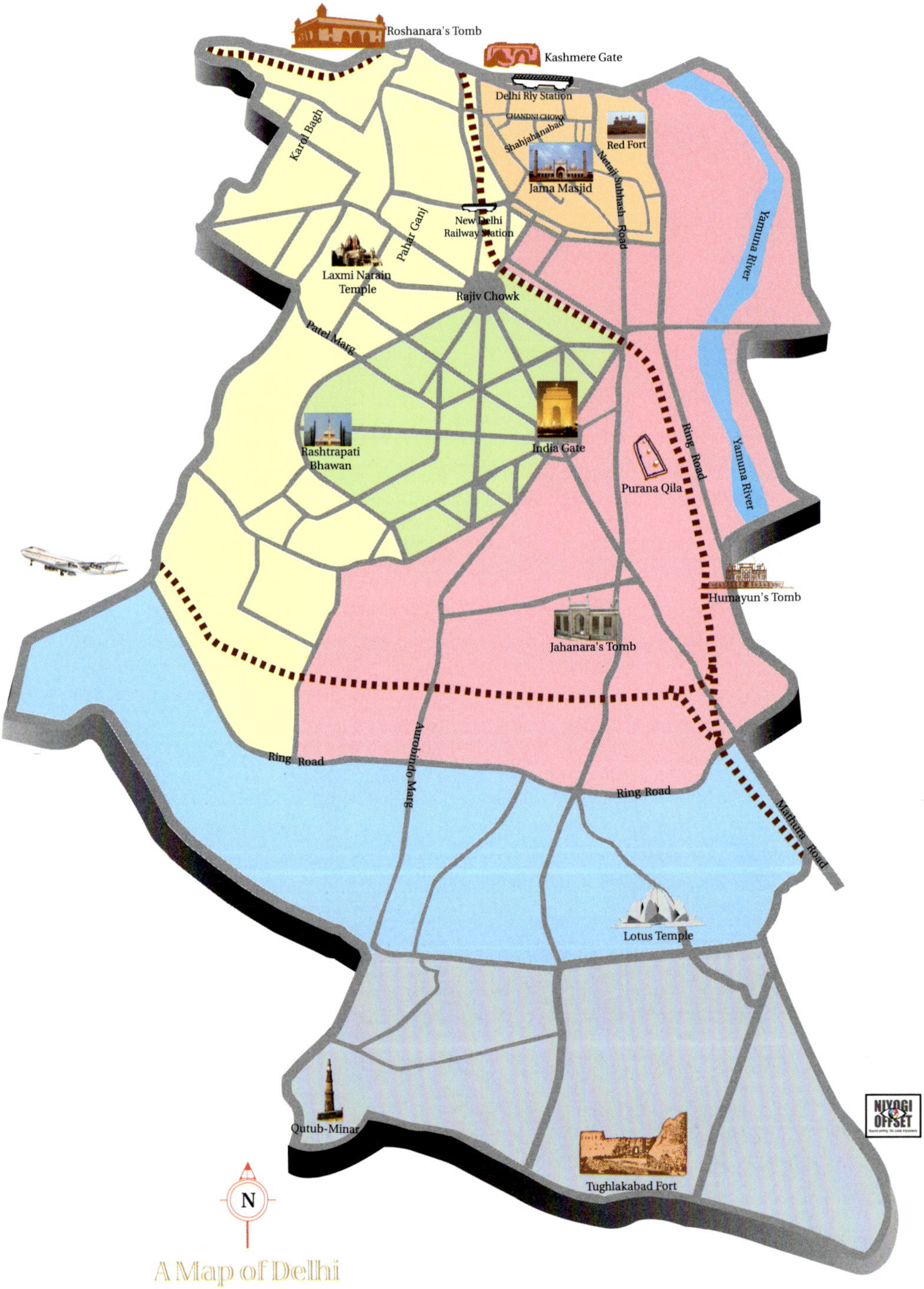

A Map of Delhi
showing the location of Jama Masjid

NOT TO SCALE

Foreword

by Professor Mushirul Hasan

Who so buildeth for God a place of worship
Be it like the nest of a Qata-bird
God buildeth for him a house in paradise

About five hundred metres west of the Red Fort stands an enduring monument to Shah Jahan's passion – the Jama Masjid, an extraordinary specimen of architectural extravaganza built during the years 1650-1656. On its completion, it symbolised the high point in Mughal architecture. The following description is useful:

> The Jumma Masjid stands upon a rocky eminence at the back of the Chandni Chouk.... "The little hill upon which it stands was originally a high conical point of rock; but no undertaking being too great for the architects of the days in which it was built, the upper part of the rock was cut away, and made serviceable in filling in below; and thus a large table surface was obtained, upon which the foundation of the present building was laid. This was executed in the year 1632 [sic], by order of Shah Jahan, then reigning, and the mosque itself, so deservedly admired by all, for its exquisite symmetry, is said to have been the emperor's own design..."
>
> (Thomas Bacon, cited in HK Kaul, ed. *Historic Delhi: An Anthology*, OUP, 1998, p. 281)

Take one of the three pyramidal flights of steps on the east, north or south leading up to the main courtyard that has a large marble tank. Here the devout wash before offering their prayer. Once you mingle with them you realise why the great mosque has become a spiritual oasis.

The grandfather of Maulvi Zakaullah, the historian at the Delhi College, died in *sijda* performing the namaz. His family believed that Allah had blessed him and ensured his place in paradise. "Mir Mahdi," wrote Mirza Ghalib in solemnity, "have you forgotten my accustomed ways? Have I ever once missed listening to the recitation of the Quran at the Jama Masjid during the blessed month of Ramzan? How could I stay in Rampur during Ramzan?"

More generally, Muhammad Iqbal describes the impact of *Azan* in the following lines:

Suddenly rose the prayer-call,
And overflowed heaven's lake;
That summons at which even
Cold hearts of mountains quake.

Again, the glory and splendour of the Masjid beckons – from sunrise to sunset – the faithful to unite in congregation and reinforces Iqbal's assertion that the slave and master perform the *namaz* under the same roof:

Ek hi saf mein khare ho gaye Mahmud-o-Ayaz
Na koi banda raha aur na koi banda nawaz

Today, the same Masjid, the theme of this richly illustrated book by Mr. NL Batra, stands majestically on top of a large hill. It symbolises many things to many people, a site of religious piety and devotion, for example. To some, it is also a vibrant symbol of secular India, a country inhabited by nearly 140 million Muslims whose religious rights are safeguarded by a constitution that is both democratic and secular. When the *muezzin* calls the faithful to prayer five times a day, scores of people hurriedly walk through the crowded bazaars to take the flight of stairs leading to the spacious courtyard of the Jama Masjid. This is a testimony of living Islam in the Indian environment.

The great mosque has witnessed the changing fortunes of Shahjahanabad, 'the Sovereign City in Mughal India' from 1639-1739. It started with the steady decline of the Mughal Empire, followed by its final dénouement. Thanks to Lord Lake, the British presence was felt in the early nineteenth century. Soon, stories of their stranglehold over Aurangzeb's inept successors began circulating in the bazaars. The anti-British pamphlet plastered on the Jama Masjid – *Risala-i Fatha-i-Islam* – offered a flicker of hope to just a handful who sought to oust the *farangis* from Shahjahanabad. But the 1857 uprising burst like a bubble.

Delhi was stormed on September 14, 1857. The minarets of Jama Masjid, a mute witness to the plight of a beleaguered Bahadur Shah, the last Mughal Emperor, saw it all. A few days later, the Masjid itself was taken over. Officers and soldiers clambered up the minaret and "saw the whole city and country like a map below our feet; all Delhi was ours". They danced about, drank beer and brandy, and lit fire in the mosque. More celebration took place at the home of Colonel Baird Smith. Midnight came, corks popped, fireworks exploded.

From the top of the Ridge an officer in the Engineering Corps gazed down at a picturesque city: the red walls and fine gateways of the palace, the splendid Jama Masjid, the red walls with the bastions, the Yamuna with its green banks; "altogether a beautiful and most interesting view". By October, many of the structures between Lal Qila and the Masjid were razed to the ground to provide the fort a clear field of fire. "Where is Delhi?" Mirza Ghalib anguished. "By God, it is not a city now. It is a camp. It is a cantonment..." "I tell you without exaggeration," he told his friend, "that from the Jama Masjid to the Rajghat Gate is a barren wilderness, and if the bricks piled here and there were taken away it would be absolutely bare." The British seized the Jama Masjid, sold the Fatehpuri Masjid to a banker, and used the Zinat-ul Masjid as a bakery. Mirza Ghalib, living in Gali Qasimjaan, bemoaned:

The walls and doorways of my house are mourning
Are as meadows overgrown with grass;
Where is the spring, why ask how the autumn looks?

The Jama Masjid remained under British occupation until 1862. To one of his friends, Ghalib reported: "News of the King's death appeared in *Awadh Akhbar*, but I've not seen it confirmed anywhere...They say that the Jama Masjid is to be given back. I shouldn't be surprised if it's true." Finally, on December 16, 1862, he informed the same friend, "You seek news of Delhi and Alwar accept my greetings. The Jama Masjid has been returned. On the steps of the Chitli Qabar side, the kabab-sellers have set up shop, and eggs and hens and pigeons are on sale."

The Masjid would have been levelled to the ground if Lord Palmerton had his way. Some wanted a Christian cathedral to be built in its place. But better sense prevailed. Canning, the British viceroy, urged the Prime Minister not to ask for anything to be done against the religion of either race. Other officials scotched the proposal to remove the tank of the Jama Masjid for the convenience of the Punjab Infantry, and ordered that the Infantry be shifted from the Masjid to the cattlesheds in Daryaganj.

Except for a flurry of activity during the Khilafat movement in the early 1920s when Swami Shraddhanand spoke from Jama Masjid's pulpit, an eloquent testimony to Hindu-Muslim amity then, life in and around the mosque remained generally quiet after the 1857 tumult. The British wielded the big stick to drive out the recalcitrant elements and reduced their detractors into submission or willing collaborators. From the 1860s onwards, the winds of the nationalist ferment did not blow across Shahjahanabad, though a few sporadic outbursts caused concern in bureaucratic circles. In general, the imperial progress became smooth and steady. This was exemplified by the state entry of King George V, crowned emperor of India on December 12, 1912. Astride a horse on a perfect winter's day with a bright sun, blue sky and cool breeze, his procession passed through Red Fort between the stately fort and the gleaming domes of Jama Masjid.

In the words of Akbar Ilahabadi, the poet:

I saw minds maddened by excitement
I too went and saw what Delhi was about
I got a good look at whatever I saw
How do I recount all that I saw?

I saw the height of the British raj
The splendour of the throne and crown
I saw the ways of today's world
And the face of the emperor Curzon.

What a great event this one
A ball in the royal fort
Every hall illuminated
The tales of the past come alive.

Yet, this elaborate and grand extravaganza turned out to be the last one. As the Indian flag fluttered on the ramparts of the Red Fort, once the site of the trial of Bahadur Shah Zafar, the last Mughal Emperor, the curtain was drawn on the British Empire. India's 'tryst with destiny' began on that midnight hour, and the nation's soul, as Jawaharalal Nehru recorded in his memorable speech, found utterance.

The author, photographer and the publisher of this book have combined well to produce this excellent pictorial book. Indeed, they have done an admirable job. Most of the photographs illustrate that the Jama Masjid is a sacred Muslim site. It will remain so in secular India. But, lest we forget, this splendid structure that has, for centuries, attracted millions, is also an integral part of our common religious and cultural inheritance. Claims of individuals and groups apart, we must all contribute to its protection and preservation. A national monument has to be looked after by the nation, by the civic and institutional bodies and not by religious trusts alone.

Preface

It is amazing that while most of the magnificent buildings constructed during the Mughal dynasty have been detailed by historians, architects and travellers to India in the past and the present, one of the finest mosques in India remains virtually undocumented and undiscovered in print. With the exception of passing references to this mosque, there does not appear to be any comprehensive book to be found on the Jama Masjid.

It is this gap that I have attempted to fill in this book, *Call of the Soul;* an exercise close to my heart that, in a sense, became both, my mission and my passion for many years.

I was fortunate to have worked at the Jama Masjid for more than a decade as part of a conservation and preservation project conducted by the Archaeological Survey of India (ASI). The organisation handles the maintenance, conservation, preservation and restoration of more than 5,000 monuments in India that are of national and historical importance. The conservation and restoration work carried out by the ASI for decades also needs to be mentioned, as it has not received the attention it richly deserves.

I have worked at the ASI for more than forty years. My early work there, in addition to the execution of restoration and conservation projects, involved the preparation of detailed drawings of every part of the Jama Masjid. This brought me closer to the mosque and my desire to write a book on the marvellous monument grew. I had earlier written a book on heritage conservation and in a way was preparing myself for this book which is indeed a call of the soul.

As the manuscript began to take shape, I realised that there is so much more to the Jama Masjid than the edifice itself. For, it is not only a place of worship or an architectural marvel or a historic monument. Its arches and domes narrate varied stories of the days gone by.

Let the pages of this book take you on a journey through the Jama Masjid, where time and tradition come together to weave a historic tale.

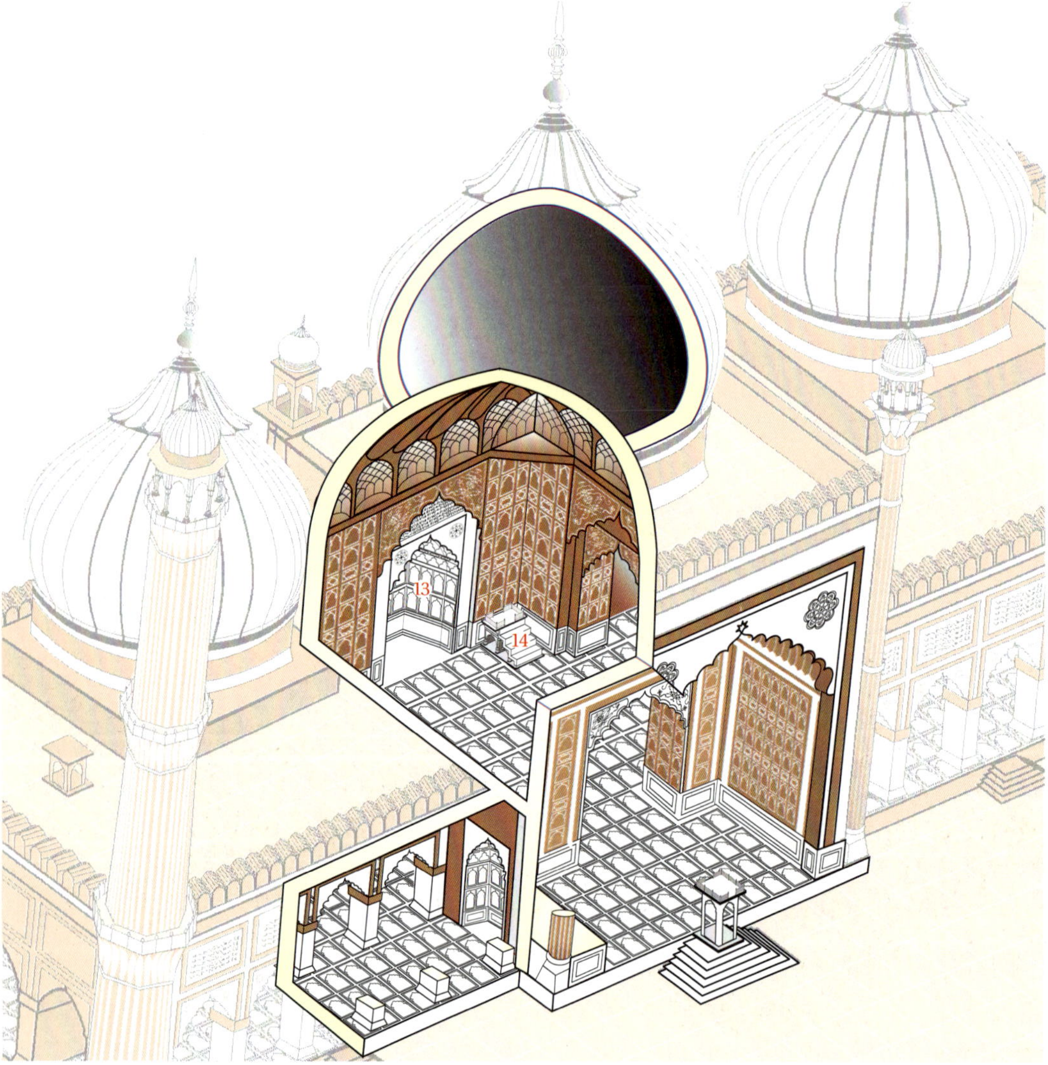

Essentia

1. Nave
2. Aisles
3. Maqsura Scree
4. Minars
5. Dome

Jama Masjid
An Architectural Marvel

The Jama Masjid's arches, domes, minars, gates and cloisters narrate its story

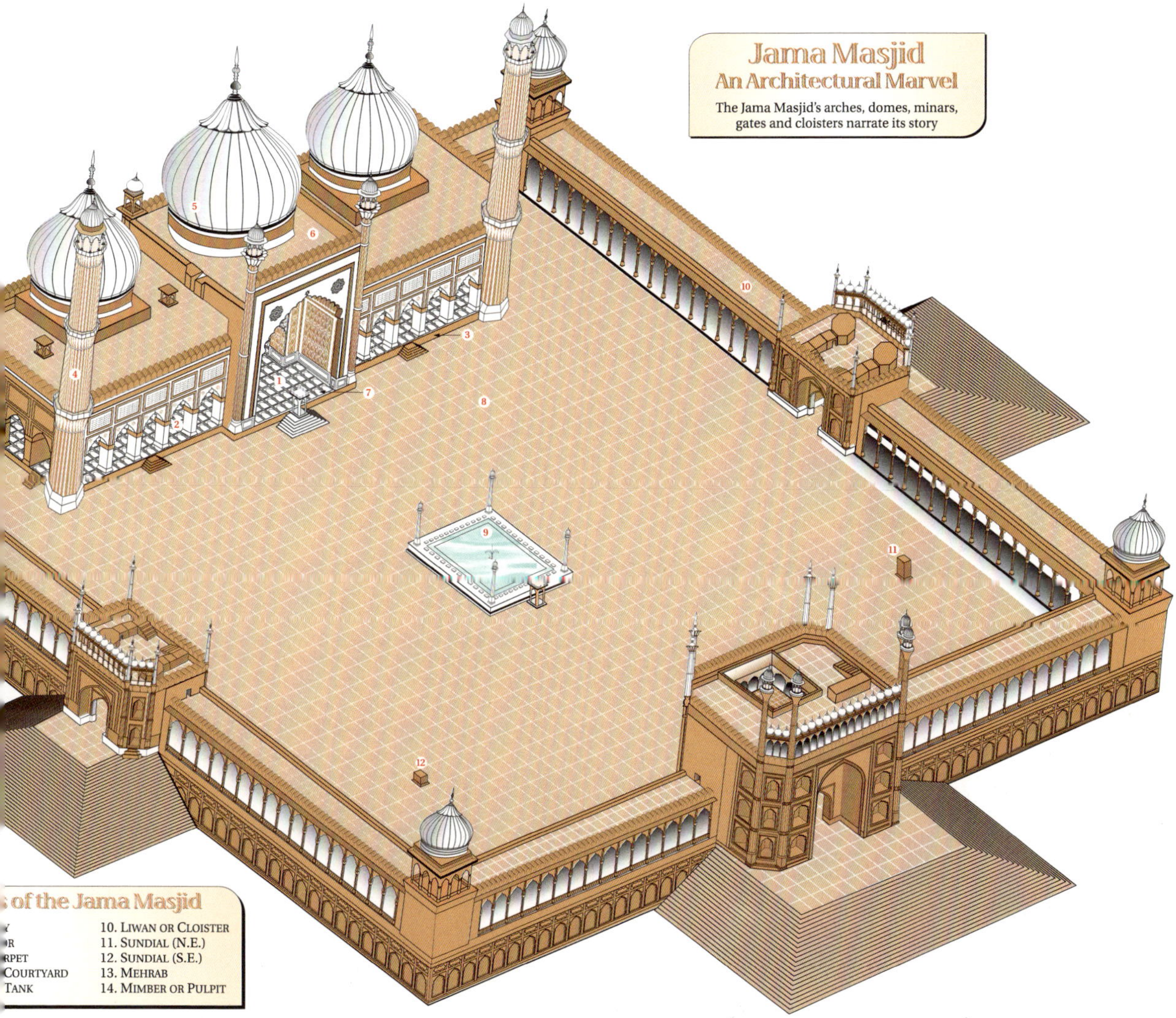

s of the Jama Masjid

Y
R
RPET
COURTYARD
TANK

10. Liwan or Cloister
11. Sundial (N.E.)
12. Sundial (S.E.)
13. Mehrab
14. Mimber or Pulpit

The Beginning

Delhi, Friday, the tenth Shawwal 1060 A.H.
(October 6, 1650 A.D.)

It is history being made. It is a moment that is being etched in red sandstone in a magnificent facade.
The arches and minarets will come alive for eternity as Mughal Emperor Shah Jahan lays the foundation stone of the finest mosque in the world.

It is believed that the day the foundation stone of the mosque was laid, people from all across Delhi, including nobles and maulvis, assembled here. Addressing the eager crowd, Shah Jahan offered anyone who had never missed a single midnight prayer the honour of laying the stone. No one came forward.

This mosque was later named the Jama Masjid (Al Masjidul Jami-lit), the collecting place for people to assemble for their Friday (Jumah) prayers. It was built under the supervision of Shah Jahan's Prime Minister Sadullah Khan and architect Fazil-mir-Saman. Over 5,000 labourers worked here daily for a period of six years, earning one pice per day.

Simplicity in structure was the intent. Artisans and sculptors, lithographers, calligraphers and engineers, brought their combined skills and talents to the creation of the wonder that is the Jama Masjid. The stone and other material used were donated by the nobles and the total cost incurred was rupees ten hundred thousand, a fortune, indeed, in those days.

The figures and the facts, the costs and the effort all seem irrelevant the moment you step into the vast and serene courtyard of the Jama Masjid. Time stands still and soon you are transported to a warm day in the year 1656 on the auspicious day of Eid-ul-Fitr when the emperor adorned the Masjid and again when people gathered here to celeberate Eid-i-Uzah with the emperor.

Turn back a few more pages and you are transported to the time when Shah Jahan came to Delhi and decided to live in the beautiful environs here. After building the fortified city of Shahjahanabad and his palace, Red Fort, on the right bank of River Yamuna, he realised the need for a large congregational mosque for public worship and for his own ceremonial usage. The location he chose for this mosque was about 500 metres west of the Red Fort and about 450 metres west of the main road from Darya Ganj to Chandni Chowk (known as Elgin Road during the British period. It is now known as Netaji Subhash Road). Its location was strategic, this was the highest point on the rocky ridge, known as Koh-Hujla thereafter known as the Bhojla Pahari, as a dacoit named Bhojla used to live here.

Southern Gate leading to the Jama Masjid

In building this mosque, Shah Jahan made an attempt to carry further the great tradition of Emperor Akbar's mosque at Fatehpur Sikri. The Jama Masjid resembles its prototype in shape with its triple domes on the sanctuary. After the completion of the mosque, Shah Jahan led a procession from Naqqar Khana of Red Fort, passing through the Delhi Gate, the principal street of the Faiz Bazaar and the Khas Bazaar, constructed during his rule. The entire route to the Jama Masjid was flanked by rows of elephants with gold and silver decorations. There were also a large number of horses, camels and musketeers, all adding to the revelries of that momentous day. The entire area had been decorated with chandeliers, prayer carpets and tapestries.

The monarch, with the accompanying pomp and splendour, entered the house of Allah through the Royal Gate on the eastern side. He then held prayers led by Imam-ul-Sultan from Bukhara who presented him with a robe of honour and other valuables. In a gesture worthy of the sobriety of the occasion, Shah Jahan conferred on him the title of Imam-ul-Sultan or Shahi Imam.

Etching of the Jama Masjid by Thomas Daniell

Francois Bernier, the noted historian, during his travel to Delhi in March-April 1659, wrote: "The King repairs to this 'Mosquee' every Friday, for the purpose of prayer, that day corresponding in Mohametan countries to our Sunday. The streets through which he passes are watered to lay the dust and temper the heat: two or three hundred musketeers form an avenue from the gate of the fortress, and as many more line both sides of a wide street leading directly to the mosque. The muskets of these soldiers are small but well-finished, and have a sort of large scarlet covering with a little streamer on the top.

Five or six horsemen, well-mounted, are also ready at the fortress gate, and their duty is to clear the way for the King, keeping, however, at a considerable distance in advance, lest he should be incommoded by their dust. These preparations completed, his Majesty leaves the fortress, sometimes on an elephant, decorated with rich trappings, and a canopy supported by painted and gilt pillars; and sometimes in a throne gleaming with azure and gold, placed on a litter covered with scarlet or brocade, which eight chosen men, in handsome attire, carry on their shoulders. A body of 'Omrahs' follow the King, some on horseback, and others in 'Palekys'; and among the 'Omrahs' are seen a great number of 'Mansebdars', and the bearers of silver maces...I cannot say that this train resembles the pompous processions, or (which is a more appropriate term) the masquerades of the Grand Seignior, or the martial retinues of European Monarchs: its magnificence is of a different character; but it is not therefore the less royal."

Historian Tavernier's description: "Emperor Aurangzeb used to proceed to the Mosque on Friday in a palanquin, with one son mounted on horseback at his side, and all the nobles of the court on foot. Four elephants with standards and four with howdahs headed the procession, and a bodyguard of 550-600 pikemen and 300-400 matchlock men accompanied it. If the king rode on horseback the nobles again walked in front, but if he went on elephant they accompanied him on horses! The following prayer (Khatbah) for the king and his people offered at public worship would be probably of great interest to the reader:

'O Lord! Do thou grant honour to the faith of Islam and to the professors of that faith through the perpetual power and majesty of thy slave, the Sultan, the son of the Sultan, the Emperor (Khakan), the son of the Emperor, the ruler of the two continents and the master of two seas, the Ghazi (the conqueror), the Mujahid (the warrior in the cause of God). The Emperor Abdul Muzaffir Shahabuddin, Muhammad Shah Jahan Ghazi – May God perpetuate his dominions and empire.

'O Lord! Defend him and his armies. Be thou his guardian, his Helper and his Defender. Give his sword the power to slay the rebellious and the wicked. 'O Lord! Give peace and rest to all cities of the Musalmans, and appoint protection, safety and health for us and for the servants, the pilgrims, the Ghazis and all Musalmans travelling by sea or land.' "

The Vision

Prince Khurram, son of Emperor Jahangir and grandson of Emperor Akbar, ascended the throne in 1628, after a brief rule in the year 1627 by Dawar Baksh, the son of Khusru, the elder brother of Prince Khurram. This thirty-five-year-old Prince had a vision that encompassed the creation of a grand empire. Adhering to this ideal, he became Shah Jahan, the Ruler of the World. A great patron of architecture, with him came the golden era of building.

That Shah Jahan loved beauty is evident from the gardens, palaces, mosques and other monuments that he created. His passion for architecture and eye for every detail ensured that his name was carved in stone for future generations to remember and revere.

Facing Page: *Portrait of Shah Jahan*

Left: *The Jama Masjid lit up*

Today, Shah Jahan is remembered most for the Taj Mahal, the famous and beautiful mausoleum that he built in Agra in 1632-1643 A.D. in memory of his beloved wife Arjumand Banu Begum, with the title of Mumtaz Mahal. It is said that Mumtaz died in Behrampur (Madhya Pradesh) in June 1631 during the long and painful birth of her youngest daughter.

Shah Jahan's contribution to art and architecture goes much beyond this. His thirty-year reign witnessed the construction of several glorious buildings that stand testimony to his vision of a grand empire, including the Jama Masjid, the finest mosque in the world.

Shah Jahan moved the seat of empire from Agra to Delhi and laid the foundation of Shahjahanabad between 1638 and 1648. The two focal points of the city were the Red Fort and the Jama Masjid.

Even today, when you enter the Jama Masjid, the call of the muezzin for prayer reverberates with the sound of an age gone by. An age when Shah Jahan lived in the Red Fort and visited the Jama Masjid for prayers and other ceremonies. An age that has been forever etched in sandstone in this marvellous mosque. Both the fort and the mosque reflect the grandeur, strength and faith prevalent in the Mughal court of those days. Days that seemed to have ended with the death of Shah Jahan and his artistic vision.

Bird's eye view of the Jama Masjid

The Evolution

Places of worship have always reflected the changing times and customs of a country. It is within their hallowed precincts that history is often created. Emperors have left their mark in the intricate arches, domes and minarets that adorn these places of worship. Standing as a testimony to this is the Quwwat-ul-Islam mosque, located in Delhi's Qutb Minar area. It is the first mosque to be built in India. This was in the year 1197 and its builder was Qutb'uddin Aibak of the Slave Dynasty.

The open space here, an essential feature of any mosque, is enclosed by a pillared verandah. A separate area to accommodate ladies was built on the first floor of the eastern entrance. An imposing screen with a lofty arch in the centre flanked by similar but shorter arches on either side facing the west, was added later, indicating the direction of Mecca.

The impressive Qutb Minar, the tallest stone tower in India, was built during this period. It adjoins the Quwwat-ul-Islam mosque and reflects the need for the muezzin to call the faithful to prayer. These minars later became regular features of a mosque. Gateways were introduced by Alauddin Khilji in 1296.

Quwwat-ul-Islam mosque, the first mosque built in India

It was customary for Muslims to offer prayers under the open sky. But with the passage of time, it was realised that an enclosed building probably provides a more serene atmosphere for worship. The Quwwat-ul-Islam mosque was thus devised in a rudimentary form, with a large open courtyard surrounded by colonnades.

Other prominent mosques built in a similar fashion, with a courtyard surrounded by colonnades, included one at Mandu, Madhya Pradesh, in District Dhar. This was built in 1405 by Dilawar Khan and has deeper aisles in the sanctuary. Similarly, at the same place, a mosque was built by Malik Mughith, Mohammed Khilji's father, in the year 1432. The style of architecture here is hybrid, where the elements of Hindu and Muslim architecture are mixed.
The effect is somewhat quaint and at a cursory glance the arched openings of the basement, the turrets of the north-east and southeast corners of the facade and the three domes of the roof appear clearly as an Islamic structure. But the columns in the sanctuary and in the colonnades are carved in Hindu fashion. The ceiling is crowned by three domes with a number of compartments built to a star-shaped plan. The roof is flat and resembles the roof of Hindu buildings. Other mosques built at Dhar in Madhya Pradesh are of the same design. Arches in India trace their origin to Muslim architecture where the cusped arch was used in the Addai-din-ka-Jhompra, in Ajmer.

It was during the Tughlaq period that separate prayer halls, purely of Muslim character, were built. The west wall was pierced by arches, surmounted by domes and flanked by minarets. Finally, it was the Qul'a-i-Quhna Masjid, built by Sher

Facing Page: *Central arch of the Adai-din-ka-Jhompra in Ajmer, flanked by cusped arches*

Left: *Central arch of the Adai-din-ka-Jhompra*

Qul'a-i-Quhna Masjid in the Purana Qila

Shah inside the citadel of Purana Qila, New Delhi, that attained a full-fledged mosque design, that is, an open space with a tank for ritual ablutions. Many of these features were later incorporated in the Jama Masjid.

Impressed by the mosques at Constantinople, the founder of the Mughal dynasty, Babar, built several mosques at Sambhal, Panipat, Rohtak, Maham, Sonepat in Haryana, and at Pilkhuwa, Agra and Ayodhya in Uttar Pradesh. His son Humayun carried on this tradition and his grandson Akbar, in his time, proved a prolific builder. His capital, Fatehpur Sikri in Agra, is considered an architectural marvel.

Akbar's grandson Shah Jahan inherited this love for art and architecture. He built three mosques, the Jama Masjid at Delhi and the Jami Masjid and Moti Masjid at Agra.
But it is the Jama Masjid in Delhi that is hailed as the most impressive mosque of the Mughal dynasty. One visit to this spectacular monument is all that it takes to verify this statement.

Offering prayers at the Jama Masjid

The Leader

A matchless mosque needs a spiritual guide worthy of its stature. After completing the construction of the Jama Masjid, Emperor Shah Jahan began his search for such a person. For this exalted post he sought a man of high qualities, well versed in Islamic scriptures, pious and noble by birth. Shah Jahan appointed a search committee who approached the ruler of Bukhara for the services of Syed Abdul Ghaffoor Bukhari, a descendant of the great saint Hazrat Jalal Bukhari.

Syed Abdul Ghaffoor Bukhari was appointed Imamat-e-uzma of the Jama Masjid, the Jahan-Numah, and the title of Imam-ul-Sultan was conferred on him. The first congregational prayer was led by him here on the day of Eid-ul-Fitr in 1656. He was also bestowed with the honour of crowning the Mughal emperors.

As the Imamat is an inherited title, the eldest son of the Imam succeeds his father. This tradition has been carried down the centuries and today, the thirteenth Shahi Imam of Jama Masjid, Syed Ahmed Bukhari, follows the illustrious path paved by his forefathers.

The Jama Masjid illuminated to mark the appointment of the thirteenth Imam

A View from the Eastern Gateway
(Author's Vision)

A majestic flight of steps leads you to the great mosque, made of red sandstone. These take you to the shrine and to your first glimpse of the marvel that is the JAMA MASJID

The Mosque

A majestic flight of steps leads you to the great mosque. Made of red sandstone, these take you to the shrine and to your first glimpse of the marvel that is the Jama Masjid.

The gate on the southern side, with its thirty-three steps, was meant for the general public and the Eastern Gate or the Royal Gate with thirty-five steps, the highest and largest one, was formally reserved for the use of the Mughal emperor. Even during the British period it was opened only to admit royal visitors and the Viceroy of India. The thirty-nine steps on the northern side lead to the Gate of Nobles.

The splendid structure stands on a rocky hill. It was covered with large hewn stones and brick masonry in lime mortar so as to smoothen its basement walls. The surface of the basement wall, which is 9.4 metres high, was adorned with false arches of red sandstone to give it a stately appearance.

Southern Gate of the Jama Masjid

Parapet of the Eastern Gate with kanjuras

The eastern gateway, or the Royal Gate, is an imposing entrance to the mosque. This is a massive, three-storeyed gate, octagonal in plan, with a large four-centred arch under an oblong panel that is recessed into its western external face. It meets the upper portion of the walls with its apex sloped inwards.

The imposing eastern gateway, with intricate honeycomb carving in the soffit of its arch

The soffit of the roof is decorated with honeycomb carving that is worked into the red sandstone itself. Its shorter sides on the facade have small false recessed arches, three in each panel. The parapet has nineteen kanjuras on the front side and each of its two shorter sides have three kanjuras. On the top is an equal number of cupolas. At each of its front angles there is an octagonal red sandstone pinnacle bearing a marble pavilion with a marble dome crowned with a white spike. Its inner dimensions are 18.29 metres wide, 15.24 metres deep and its height is 15.24 metres.

Wooden gate overlaid with brass arabesques

Jharokha over the inner arch of the eastern gateway

Its eastern face consists of one large archway with three arched openings on adjacent sides. The shorter sides also have three arched openings. There are doors under these arches and steps that lead to the upper compartments.

Above the central inner archway is a projected balcony, or aerial window, crowned by three marble domes. It is said to have been used as a pulpit. This window provides the only ornamentation to this side of the gateway. The balcony bears the influence of the Bengali style of architecture where such carved features were made by the innovative use of bent bamboo. The Bengalis mainly used timber, bamboo, reed, straw or bricks as their building material. Bamboo provides a curved element that is unique to their style and is used for decorating cornices and chajjas. This aspect of Hindu architecture has found its way into many Mughal buildings across north India. These curved features also appear in the square throne pavilion of the Diwan-e-Am of the Red Fort.

The surface of the walls is decorated with an arched effect. The marble inlay work laid in the red sandstone adds another touch of beauty to the monumental building. The doors of this gateway are of wood, about three inches thick, and are overlaid with half-inch thick brass arabesques.

The steps of the eastern gateway were generally used by sellers of poultry, who carried bird cages. It formed a picturesque sight: sellers of pigeons on one side of the steps, and those selling horses on the other side. There was drama and there was colour. And the Jama Masjid stood a silent spectator.

Smaller than the eastern gateway, the northern and the southern gateways are double-storeyed and shaped like irregular octagons. Their main arches spring from a plinth, less than one metre high, and are recessed into a small entrance arch. They have an embattled parapet and are crowned by kiosks with white marble domes and spikes.

On the front are four tapering, ornamental marble pinnacles with floral heads and white spikes. Two

View of the inner facade of the eastern gateway

similar pinnacles are on the back, emerging from the roof. The front walls of these gateways are decorated with interlacing geometrical and arch patterns with white marble inlay work in the red sandstone. There are in all four huzrahas, two on the ground floor and two on the first. The access to these rooms and the top of the gateways is from the two inner wings of the gateways. The back facade of these gateways is shorter than its front.

The northern steps were formerly occupied by cooks and bakers, jugglers and groups listening to professional storytellers. The southern steps were generally frequented by cloth merchants. Sellers of sherbet, faluda and kababs were the main occupants of these steps. People gathered here to enjoy these delicacies and to meet each other, contributing further to the hustle and bustle that was an intrinsic charm of this area.

The cloisters on the north and south are also similar. There are seventeen arched openings on each side of the gateway of which three arches in each wing are closed, forming the small rooms used as a store by the Jama Masjid authorities. Similarly, on the eastern side, there are fifteen arched

A marble water tank, with the northern gateway and cloisters in the background

openings on either side of the gateway. Three arches on these sides are closed in order to store the material required for the maintenance of the Masjid.

On the west there are five arched openings on either side of the main sanctuary or mosque hall. The arches of these cloisters are supported by red sandstone pillars with floral patterns. The top of these arches are shaded with wide eaves or chhajjas, crowned by an embattled parapet. These were built as a protection from the harsh rays of the sun. At each of its corners are hujrahs and on the top of each hujrah stands an open square pavilion crowned by white marble domes and copper gilt spikes.

An open courtyard, a sahn or livan, measuring 109.75 metres by 109.75 metres, is bound on three sides by cloisters that are 6.7 metres wide. In the centre of this courtyard is a marble tank, 30.71 metres by 10.96 metres, that is used for ritual ablution where the devout wash their hands and faces before offering prayers. In the centre of the tank is a fountain which now needs to be made functional. Ornamental white marble pillars crowned with kiosks placed in its four corners were later additions.

The tank was fed by a well outside, on the southern side, which is now lost to view because of changes in the surrounding

The faithful walking over the cloister

area. This well was repaired in 1803 by Archibald Seton, the then British Resident. The northwestern corner of the tank was marked by an enclosure as the seat of the Messenger of Allah in 1766. This is believed to be the spot where the Prophet appeared to Mohammad Tahsin Muhali Badshai, a devotee.

A marble water tank for ritual ablutions

کوثر محمد رسول الله

۱۱۸۰

(۱) رسول دیده اند اینجا ولی و اهل الله   بجاست گر شود این سنگ هم زیارتگاه

(۲) بنای سال به تحسین و آفرین هاتف   بگفت احاطه جای نشست رسول الله

۱۱۸۰

باني جای ادب داعي محمد تحسین محلی بادشاهي

"Kausar [the name of a spring in Paradise] of Muhammad, the messenger of God."

"Saints and the people of God have seen the Prophet here; it is proper if this stone also should become a place of pilgrimage."

"The year of its construction, the invisible voice said with praise and applause, 'The enclosure of the seat of the messenger of God'."

"The founder of the place of respect, Muhammad Tahsim, the royal eunuch, who prays for blessings. 1180."

At the central entrance to the mosque is a grey sandstone pulpit that is used as a seat for the Mukabbir, the person who assists the Imam by announcing the time during which the various motions in the prayer are regulated. This was erected in 1829 by Mirza Salim, son of Akbar II.
In front of the tank is a raised sandstone platform erected at a later stage for the use of the muezzin.

Central arch of sanctuary with a raised pulpit, a seat for the Mukabbir

Sundial

Pillar with sundial

Locations of holy relics and sundial

At the northeast and southeast corners of the courtyard are low pillars. On these are fixed marble slabs. The eastern hemisphere is carved on one and, on the other, certain hour lines are marked. Each has an upright iron spike. The shadow cast by the sun on this indicates the time for prayers.

An enclosed part of the northeast corner contains holy relics, carefully preserved through the centuries. These include the twenty-eighth chapter of the Quran written by Ali, the husband of Muhammad's daughter Fatima; the fifteenth chapter of the Quran written by Hussain, the son of Fatima and Ali; Kafsh Mubarak, the slipper worn by Muhammad; Mue-Mubarak, a strand of red hair from Muhammad's beard and Kadam-Mubarak, an impression of Muhammad's foot in marble.

These relics are said to have been brought by Timur from Medina. They were formerly kept at the northwestern end of the mosque in an enclosure with a red sandstone screen, built by a nobleman in the era of Alamgir II who described himself in an inscription as the slave, the faithful, the clean-hearted Ilmas Khan.

Enclosure where the holy relics are preserved

He wrote the following words in an inscription on the screen:

(۱) پیش آثار مبارک سرور آخر زمان
در زمان شاه عالمگیر خاقان جهان
(۲) با سیادت ساخت دیوار حجر از سنگ سرخ
بندهٔ با اعتقاد از صدق دل الماس خان
(۳) سال تاریخ بنا چون میر جست از عقل و هوش
گفت هاتف بهر خود را کرده ابواب جنان

"In front of the blessed relics of the chief of the last age (the Prophet Muhammad) during the time of Shah Alamgir, the king of the world, with greatness a wall of red stone was built, with a true heart, by the faithful slave Ilmas Khan. When Mir asked Thought and Intelligence the year of its erection, an invisible voice said, 'He has opened for himself the doors of Paradise."

This inscription is kept elsewhere in the mosque. Visitors to the Jama Masjid can request to see these relics even today. Carefully preserved, venerated with rose petals, a glimpse of these relics is translated into a sublime moment that brings one closer to eternity.

The holy Quran

Namazi reading a holy book

Kadam-Mubarak, an impression of Hazrat Mohammad's foot

The holy relic

View from the front gate

On the west side of the court is the Ibadat Khana, a prayer hall, a large and imposing building. It is also known as the mosque sanctuary. Although the area occupied by the Masjid is large, the main structure, the shrine occupies a relatively small portion of the architectural scheme. The plan of the main mosque takes the form of a rectangle 79.5 metres in length and 27.4 metres in depth, with a plinth of 1.52 metres. The main entrance to this shrine is through an archway with a vaulted ceiling inlaid with alternating strips of white marble, on the apex of which is decorated a pattern inspired by the rays of the sun. The main arch is flanked by minarets surmounted by octagonal cupolas and then further flanked by ten engrailed arches of white marble. These are supported by white marble rectangular pillars enriched with inlaid floral work. It is flanked by two lofty tapering minarets, 39.6 metres high, with an octagonal base, striped vertically with marble and red sandstone. These minarets are divided by three projecting galleries and surmounted at the top by octagonal domed pavilions. Over these arches are tablets or panels of white marble, inlaid in black slate with inscriptions documenting the history of the mosque and glorifying the reign of Shah Jahan. Inscribed on the spandrel of the central arch are the words 'Ya Hadi' (the One who shows the right path), one of the ninety-nine names of Allah.

Among the different types of Muslim surface ornaments are inscriptions of text consisting of extracts from the Quran

Interior hall of main sanctuary (Ibadat Khana)

Portion of the hall adjoining the main entrance

in the stiff characters known as 'kafie', derived from its origin at Kufa. The letters are intertwined with conventional foliage to form ornamental panels. The minar consists of three storeys. Each storey is bisected by a projecting gallery, octagonal in plan and with a balustrade railing around it. Winding steps lead to the top of this elegant minar.

The story goes that there was a foreigner lying in the courtyard. People rushed to him, thinking that he had fainted in the afternoon sun. But he was only gazing at the perfect minarets. He was deeply impressed with their splendour and unique construction and claimed that if these minarets were ever to fall, Allah forbid, they would land in the courtyard and not on the prayer halls, owing to the slight slant but not noticed by most.

The main shrine is divided into two halls, one adjoining its main entrance hall and the other its interior portion. These are divided into seven bays by ornamental pillars, the general effect being that of a beautifully spaced out pavilion. The rear wall is sunk in the centre with a mihrab. It is also flanked by mihrabs in smaller sizes, three on each side. The spandrels of these mihrabs are enriched with inlay floral design. The foliated arches are the leading motif on the walls and the pillars.

Close to the central mihrab is a white marble pulpit that can be reached by

Pulpit or mimber

A view of domes and minarets

four balustraded steps. This pulpit is said to have been cut out of a single block of marble. The floor of the mosque is decorated with black marble. This is an imitation of the mosalla (the prayer carpet). It has a thin black marble border and eight-hundred-and- ninety-nine divisions, each of which is three feet long and one-and-a-half feet in width.

The Jama Masjid has many interesting architectural features. Among them are its domes, minarets, arches and pinnacles. Each has been crafted with care; each is special in its own way.

The dome is an intrinsic feature of Muslim architecture. The first experiment to build a dome in India was probably conducted during the time of Alauddin Khilji. Subsequently Hindu craftsmen adopted similar techniques. In the case of the Jama Masjid, a bulbous double dome was introduced. The inner and outer shells had sufficient space between them. This system serves adual purpose: it helps cool the interior and gives the raised outer dome a voluminous and elegant look. Here, the method employed in the construction of the inner dome is that of the squinch system where the square shape of the compartment below is united with the circular base of the dome above.

The use of minars has been debated over the centuries. Were they built to serve

The floor is designed like a mosalla (prayer carpet)

Squinch supporting the dome

as muzinah (a minar from where the faithful were summoned)? Or were they essential features of the mosque, used to impress grandeur upon the imagination of the people? Both schools of thought have their followers. Yet, at the Jama Masjid, it is clear that minars contribute significantly to its grandeur and beauty.

Also adding to its inherent splendour are the arches that adorn the Masjid. Arches in India trace their origin to Muslim architecture where the cusped arch was used in Addai-din-ka-Jhompra, in Ajmer, during the reign of Iltutmish. But this feature gained perfection only during Shah Jahan's time.

The main central hall is covered with a vaulted roof, supported by pillars and squinches. It is decorated in the centre with a floral ornament and concentric rings. The roof of this hall is further adorned with a dome that is supported by a lofty drum-shaped structure.

A dome of white marble, inlaid with vertical strips of black marble, rises to form the foliated base of the white marble finial with copper gilt spike. It is the shape and volume of this double dome that glorifies the elevation of the mosque. The two smaller domes add further elegance to the beauty of this mosque. The rest of the bays are covered with flat roofs with cavities to keep the interior cool.

At the back of the mosque, the high projected wall behind the central mihrab is flanked on each side by a pinnacle with a splayed head, on which stands an octagonal pavilion with a marble dome and gilt spike. There is also a square pinnacle at each of its ends.

The welcoming steps, the majestic gateways, red sandstone offset by pristine white marble, the decorative arches and towering minarets, all combine to enhance the austere dignity of the Jama Masjid.

Southwest view of the Jama Masjid

Gate No.1
باب عبدالله

View from the Southern side

The Words

Eleven arches adorn the front view of the mosque. Over each is a panel of white marble, inlaid in black slate, with inscriptions. These tell us the history of the mosque and glorify the reign of its creator. On the central arch is inscribed, in Tughra characters, 'Ya Hadi' (the One who shows the right path), or one of the ninety-nine names of Allah, the Great. The remaining ten arches, beginning from the north, have verses carved in them.

The main mosque with eleven arches with panels or tablets of white marble, inlaid in black slate with inscriptions

Arch I

بفرمان شهنشاه جهان پادشاه زمین و زمان گیهان خدیو کشورستان گیتي خداوند گردون
توان موسس قوانین عدل و سیاست مشید ارکان ملک و دولت بسیار دان عالي فطرت قضا فرمان
قدر قدرت فرخنده راے مجسته منظر فرخ طالع بلند اختر اسمان حشمت انجم سپاه خورشید
عظمت فلک بارگاه

By the order of the Emperor of the world, king of the earth and the age, lord of the world, conqueror of kingdoms, master of the world, powerful as the sky, founder of the laws of justice and administration, strengthener of the pillars of state and wealth, well-knowing, of exalted nature, whose commands are like the decree of fate, and position like that of Providence, of happy intellect, and auspicious appearance, fortunate and lucky, having grandeur like the firmament, soldiers (as numerous) as stars, glory like the sun and a court as spacious as the sky.

Arch II

مظهر قدرت الهي مورد كرامت نامتناهي مظهر كلمة الله العليا مروج الملة الحنيفية
البيضا ملجاء الملوك والسلاطين خليفة الله في الارضين الخاقان الا عدل الاعظم والقا ان الاجل الاكرم
ابو مظفر شهاب الدين محمد صاحبقران ثاني شاهجهان پادشاه غازي لا زالت رايات دولته منصورة
و اعداء حضرته مقهورة كه ديده بصيرت حق بينش از شعشه انوار هدايت انما يعمر مساجد الله

The manifestation of the Almighty's power, the recipient of unlimited blessings, the proclaimer of the great word of God, the promulgator of the bright faith of Hanifa [Abu Hanifa Numan, the son of Sabit of Kufa, was one of the four great expounders of Muslim law and religion], the asylum of princes and kings, the deputy of God on earth, the just and great king, the great and glorious Lord (named) Abu-l-Muzaffar Shibab-ud-Din Muhammad Sahibqiran-i-sani (the second Lord of happy conjunction) Shah Jahan Badshah Ghazi (the king and champion of faith); may the flags of his kingdom ever remain victorious, and the enemies of his Majesty subdued, whose eye of God seeing perception is lighted up by the radiance of the lights of guidance of Verily, he populates mosques of God...

Arch III

من آمن بالله واليوم الاخر مستنير است و آئينۀ ضمير صدق گزينش از اشعه مشكات
روايت احب البلاد الى الله مساجدها فروغ پذير اين مسجد كوه اساس گردون مماس كه كريمۀ
لمسجد اسس على التقوى بيان بنيان پائدار اوست و بينه و القى فى الارض رواسى ان تميد بكم
كتابۀ ايوان استوار او قمۀ و قبۀ فلك شانش از طبقات آسمان گذشته و شرفه طاق سپهر نشانش
بارج كيوان پيوسته

Who believes in God and the last day, and the mirror of whose truth adopting conscience has received light from the flame of the lamp of the tradition. The places most loved by God are mosques; this mosque with its foundation, as firm as a mountain, and as lofty as the firmament, which has for the description of its strong foundation the noble verse. Verily the mosque founded on piety, and the clear verse. The mountains were cast into the earth in order to make it firm for the inscription of its strong hall; whose sky-like pinnacle and dome have gone beyond the folds of the firmament, and the cornice of whose sky-like vaults has reached the height of Saturn.

Arch IV

(۱) گرز طاق و قبهٔ مقصوره اش جوئی نشان
هیچ نتوان گفت غیر از کهکشان و آسمان
(۲) فرد بودے قبه گر گردون نبودے ثانیش
طاق بودے طاق گر جفتش نبودے کهکشان
فروغ شمسه پیش طاق جهان نمایش روشنی بخش مصابیح سموات پرتو کلس گنبد عالم
آرایش نور افزائے قنادیل جنات منبر سنگ مرمرش چون صخره مسجد اقصی مرقات

If you want to know what the vault and cupola of its prayer chamber are like, nothing can be said except that they resemble the milky way and sky.

The dome would have been matchless, had the firmament not been its equal, the vault would have been unique had the milky way not been its pair.

The brilliance of the Shamsa (literally, a figure resembling the sun; its secondary meaning is an ornament. Here, it denotes a figure used as a decoration on the keystone of an arch) of whose world showing arch gives light to the lamps of heavens (that is, stars), the reflection of the pinnacle of whose world adorning dome increases the light of the chandelier of Paradise, whose marble pulpit, like the rock of Solomon's temple, is a ladder to…

Arch V

مقام قاب قوسین او ادنی محراب فیض گسترش مانند صبح صادق کشاده پیشانی بشارت
رسان ولقد جاء هم من ربهم الهدے ابواب رحمت ایابش صلاے و الله یدعو الی دارالسلام بمسامع
خاص و عام رسانیده منار سپهر مدارش نداے و یجزی الذین احسنوا بالحسنی از نه رواق گنبد
فیروزه‌فام گذرانیده سقف رفیع باصفایش تماشا گاه روحانیان کره افلاک

The point of Qaba Qausain au adna [literally meaning the place of two bows' length or nearer than that; this is a reference to the close proximity of the Prophet to God when he ascended the heavens from Sakhra, a rock that is on Mirqat, a staircase in Masjid-i-Aqsa – Solomon's temple], whose grace-spreading Mihrab, like the true and broad foreheaded dawn gives the good news. Verily there has come to them from their God the right path, whose doors, which are the resort of mercy, have brought to the hearing of great and small the announcement: "And God invites to the abode of peace", whose minars, which are the orbits of heavens, have sent the call: "(God) will compensate those who do good with goodness," beyond the nine folds of the blue-coloured dome (sky), whose lofty and polished roof is the pleasure ground of the spirits of the celestial sphere...

Arch VI

Central Arch(facing page)

يا هادي

'Ya Hadi'
(one of the ninety-nine names of God)

Arch VII

صحن وسیع دلکشایش سجده‌گاه پاک نژادان معمورهٔ خاک روح فضائے فیض انتما و طیب
هوائے روح افزایش از روضهٔ رضوان حکایت کرده و عذوبت ماء معین حوض دلنشین نظافت امایش
از چشمهٔ سلسبیل خبر داده در روز جمعه دهم شهر شوال ۱۰۶۰ سال هزار و شصت هجری موافق
سال چهارم از دور سیوم جلوس میمنت مانوس بساعت خجسته

Whose spacious and pleasant courtyard is the place of worship of the pure-born of this terrestrial and populated world, and the favourable refreshing good and soul strengthening air thereof resembles (the breeze of) the garden of Paradise, the sweetness of the pure water of whose pleasing and purifying tank represents the spring of Salsabil [the name of a spring in Paradise], on Friday, the tenth of the month of Shawwal of the year one thousand and sixty Hijra, corresponding to the fourth year of the third cycle of the auspicious reign, at the propitious moment.

Arch VIII

و طالع شایسته سرمایه ابتنا و پیرایه تاسیس یافت و در عرض مدت شش سال بحسن
سعي کار پردازان کاردان کارگذار و فرط اعتنا و اهتمام کار فرمایان صاحب اقتدار و بذل جد و جهد
استادان ماهر دانشور و وفور کوشش پیشه‌کاران چابک دست صاحب هنر و انفاق مبلغ ده لک
روپیه صورت انجام و طراز اختتام پذیرفت و مقارن اتمام در روز عید فطر

And the fortunate time obtained the wealth of foundation and ornament of stability, and during the period of six years, with the efficient exertions of expert and skilful workmen, with the great application and devotion of respectable superintendents, with the hearty efforts of sagacious and wise masters, and with the great exertions of apt-handed and skilled artificers at a cost of ten lakhs of rupees, obtained the form of completion and the feature of finish. Soon after its completion, on the day of Eid-ul-Fitr [the festival celebrated at the end of Ramzan].

Arch IX

بفر قدوم اقدس پادشاه ظل الله صافي نيت خدا آگاه زيب و زينت گرفت و باقامت
نماز عيد و اداے وظايف اسلام چون مسجدالحرام در روز عيد اضحي مرجع طوايف انام گرديد و
مباني اسلام و ايمان را متانت و اصانت كرامت فرمود سياحان ربع مسكون و مسالك نوردان كوه
و هامون را اراسته عمارتے باين رفعت و حصانت در آئينۂ بصر

It was adorned and embellished by the magnificence of the holiest steps of the king, the shadow of God, pure-intentioned, and God-knowing; and on the day of Eid-ul-Zuha [the festival of sacrifice, celebrated two months and ten days after Eid-ul-Fitr] it became the resort of the crowds of people, by his (the King's) saying the Eid prayers and discharging the exercise of Islam as (is done) in Masjidul-Haram (Kaba), and blessed the foundations of Islam and faith with firmness and strength. To those who have made the tour of the inhabited fourth portion (of the globe) and travellers (traversing) mountains and woods, an adorned building of such loftiness and strength have never been reflected in the mirror of their sight.

Arch X

و مرات خیال مرتسم نگشته و حقایق گذاران و قایع دهر و فکرت پردازان نظم و نثر را که
سوانح نگاران بدایع ارباب ملک و دولت و صنایع شناسان اصحاب مکنت و قدرتند افراخته بناے
باین شکوه و عظمت بر زبان قلم و قلم زبان نگذشته فرازنده کاخ هستي و طرازنده بلندي و پستي
این بنیان رفیع را که قرةالعین بینش و زینت بخش کارخانه آفرینش است

And the looking glass of their imagination, nor to the relators of the events of the age and the careful students of prose and poetry, who are the biographers of the important personages of the country and kingdom, and are the connoisseurs of the persons of might and power, has a lofty edifice of such grandeur and magnificence been brought on the tongue of their pen and the pen of their tongue. May the builder of the mansion of life and the designer of high and low places keeping this exalted building firm, which is like the pupil of the eye of sight, and the embellisher of the workhouse of creation.

Arch XI

پائدار داشته صدائے تسبیح مسبحانش را هنگامه آرائے ذاکران مجامع ملکوت و زمزمه
تهلیل مهللانش را نشاط افزائے معتکفان جوامع جبروت داراد و رؤس منابر معمورۂ جهانرا
بخطبۂ دولت جاوید طراز این پادشاه دادگر دین پرور که بمیامن ذات مقدس مبارکش ابواب
امن و امان بر روے روزگار کشاده است آراسته داراد بحق الحق و اهله - کتبه نور الله احمد -

Continue the sound of the repeaters of the praises of God on a rosary, in it, giving grace to the noise of the assembly of God praising angels, and the melodious voice of the readers of the Muhammadan creed and the name of God, in it, increasing joy of the congregations of recluse angels of the highest order, and decorate the heads of the pulpits of the inhabited world with the Khutba [an address or sermon delivered by the Imam on the occasion of Eid and Friday prayers. It contains the name of the reigning monarch] of the eternity adorning reign of this king who is an administrator of justice and a cherisher of faith, and by the blessings of whose august and holy person the doors of peace and security have been opened for the world, for the sake of God and His people.

(English renderings of inscriptions on arches by Nurullah Ahmed)

Inscribed arches to the south of the central arch

Inscribed arches to the north of the central arch

The Change

Time takes its toll on everything, even on a work of art as majestic as the Jama Masjid. Wear and tear is an intrinsic part of the history of a monument and this mosque is no exception. It was under the care of the Shahi Imams that all repairs were carried out. This tradition was followed till the British came to power in India.

The Jama Masjid was repaired in 1817 by King Akbar II. The northern minar and the stone pavement of the courtyard were damaged owing to lightning and they were repaired in 1833 and again, almost two decades later, by the British Government.

The Jama Masjid stands majestically on top of a large hill

The War of Independence of 1857 left its mark on the mosque that was considerably damaged during this period. On September 14, 1857, the besieging forces reached the Jama Masjid. They found its entrances bricked up and its gates closed. The enemy fired from the rooftops of adjacent houses. But gun powder ran short and more ammunition had not yet arrived. The attacking forces therefore receded to Begum Bagh. The Masjid ultimately fell to the victorious army led by the Delhi Field Force.

The Jama Masjid during the nineteenth century

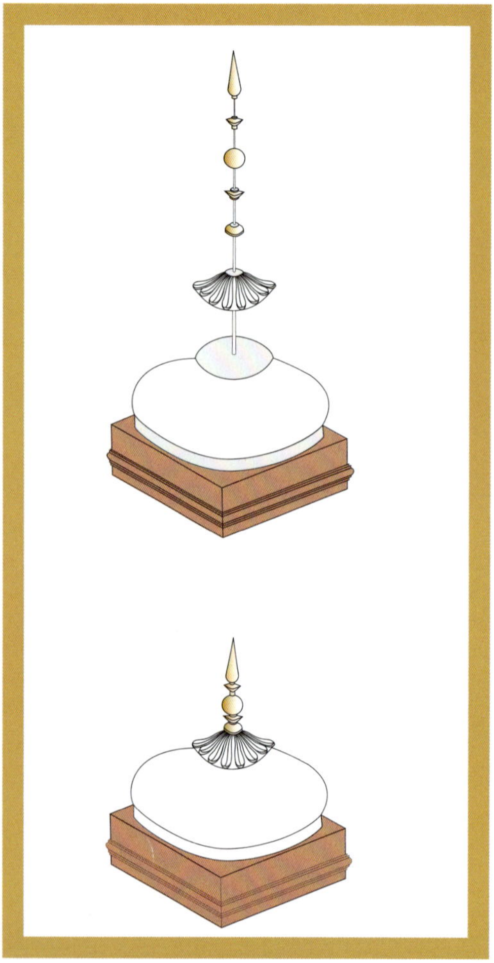

The Nawab of Rampur contributed Rs 118,000 towards the repairs that were essential at that point in time.
The Nawab of Bhawalpur also donated a smaller amount in 1900.

It was not only the ravages of war that affected the structure of this grand mosque. The forces of nature, too, combined to erode its beauty. The white marble stone used in the domes and at other places was severely affected by atmospheric pollution.

The iron used in fastening the stones also corroded over time and damage was further caused by the growth of vegetation in the core of the masonry, especially on the top of the domes in the corners of the mosque.

Dome under restoration

Another cause of damage to the stones was the smoke emitted by the coal fires by power stations situated in the vicinity. The formation of sulphuric acid resulted in the deterioration of the outer surface of the stones that subsequently blistered and flaked off, causing exfoliation.

The sandstones discoloured over time and assumed a drab appearance owing to the fact that the pores of the surface of these stones got clogged with soot and dirt. Another reason for decay was the fact that there were two dissimilar stones, sandstone and limestone, used in the construction of the mosque. Decay in the stones was also caused due to frost and an extensive use of wrought iron.

Gateway under restoration

There has been a strong desire and commitment to preserve, protect and maintain the grandeur of the mosque. Repairs and maintenance work was taken up as and when needed. It is these layers of care through the centuries that have kept the appearance of the Jama Masjid as spectacular today as originally conceived.

Top: *Dilapidated basement wall before restoration*

Bottom: *Central arch of the main sanctuary during restoration*

Facing page: *Northern minar after restoration*

The Return

The maintenance of the Jama Masjid was in the hands of a trust, Sunni-Majlis Auqaf. The Shahi Imam of Jama Masjid, however, approached the Government of India to take up the major repairs of this mosque. The trust, owing to a paucity of funds, was not able to carry out the repairs. Thus, on the instructions of the then Prime Minister Pandit Jawaharlal Nehru and the then Education Minister, a committee was formed to examine the repairs that were needed. It was decided to prepare the necessary estimate.

The committee, after careful consideration and study, submitted its report in October 1953. The conservation work was handed over to the Archaeological Survey of India (ASI) in 1955.

Minar before restoration

The restoration work began in February 1956. The plinth stones in the eastern half of the southern wing were replaced.

Marble cupolas on the gateway before restoration

The veneer stones were reset in mortar with copper clamps secured in position by lead joints. The southern gate, where most of the stones had been badly damaged due to moisture, was also attended to. Some of the stones were removed and before the new ones were placed, the decayed masonry in the brick work at the back was chiselled, the joints cleaned, the cracks grouted and the cavities filled with fresh mortar. During the following year, the facing slabs of red sandstone were replaced on the southern basement of the south and north gateways and on the pillars and

Minar after restoration

pilasters of the corridors. On the southern gateway, some new frieze stones carved with floral designs were fixed.

Marble cupolas during restoration

Weatherworn stones were being constantly identified and replaced. Joints and cracks were filled with liquid cement mortar and made watertight. The dislodged stones of the arches and pillars of the western basement were restored and also the loose stones in the interior and the northern facade of the eastern side of the southern gateway. The central dome was reset and the broken stones were replaced with new ones. Similarly, the open joints and cracks in the minar towards the northeast of the mosque were repaired and grouted with liquid

Basement wall during restoration

cement and kankar lime. The decayed red sandstones were replaced by new ones and the dislodged white marble stones on the top of the minar restored. The white marble railing on the top storey was refixed in its original place. The damaged stones of the squinches, including the ornamental panels of the main prayer chamber, were replaced.

Restoration work of the mosque carried out in the 1960s included the installation of guldastas of white marble on the southern gateway of the mosque. Red sandstone and white marble, the two main ingredients that went into the making of this great mosque in 1650, were replenished as, where and when necessary. The endeavour was always to restore the impressive appearance of the Jama Masjid.

The seventies saw extensive repair work on the white marble pillars with special mortar and further replacing of decayed stones in the verandahs and the main prayer chamber. Fixing the new red sandstone in exactly the same shape and texture as the original was a tedious process. It needed both, attention to

Left top: *Mutakkas before restoration*

Left middle: *A chhajja before restoration*

Left bottom: *A chhajja after restoration*

Top: *Inner face of southern gateway during restoration*

detail and commitment to reviving the grandeur of the mosque.

In the eighties, the repair of the ornamental black marble inlay work was carried out using special lime mortar. The terrace was given a fresh lime concrete coat. Decayed and damaged veneer stones in the chhajjas and cornices were replaced with new Tantpur ones, similar to the original colour and texture.

The Jama Masjid has been getting the attention it richly deserves, enabling it to withstand the vagaries of nature and stand proud and tall, a silent witness to the changing centuries.

Facing Page: *Outer face of southern gateway during restoration*

Top: *Base of a pillar before restoration*

Bottom: *Base of the same pillar after restoration*

The Skyline

It was during the reign of Emperor Shah Jahan, a compulsive builder by nature, that the Mughal style of architecture reached its zenith. With him came the golden era of marble. In fact, his passion for marble was so great that he even got some earlier sandstone buildings dismantled, in order to substitute them with fine marble. These include the Jahangiri Mahal and Khas Mahal at Agra Fort. Shah Jahan also added edifices in Diwan-e-Am, Diwan-e-Khas, Sheesh Mahal, the Nagina Masjid and Mussamman Burj. The Moti Masjid or Pearl Mosque is another tribute to the great builder and his love of marble.

The beautiful city of Shahjahanabad by the River Yamuna

Front view of the Red Fort

Although Shah Jahan had beautified his capital city of Agra with splendid palaces and magnificent monuments, he still felt the urge to build more. Also, the heat of Agra, coupled with the fact that its streets were congested, led him to consider other options. So he decided to move his capital to Delhi.

The Emperor is said to have summoned the Meri-i-Imarat (supervisor of buildings) and told him that he wished to live in Delhi. Two master masons, Ustad Hamid and Ustad Hira of Delhi, were, therefore, hired to construct a big fort, with palaces for the Emperor and all his queens. The land near the River Yamuna was identified for its proximity to water and soil that was free from minerals. Delhi's skyline was about to undergo a complete transformation – one that would make it a historical and elegant capital for a Mughal Emperor!

The foundation of the grand Red Fort was laid on the night of Friday, the nineteenth Moharram, of the year 1049 A.H.–May 1639. Oblong in plan, about

Naubat or Nakkar-Khana

945.12 metres long from north to south and 503 metres wide from east to west, the fort is fortified throughout with red sandstone of the Tantpur variety. It has two main gateways, one in the middle of the long side on the west and another on the southern side known as the Lahori Gate and the Delhi Gate, respectively. Within the fort,the main entrance to the Fort lies through the Lahori Gate and the palaces are reached through a roofed passage flanked by arcaded apartments called Chhata Chowk and now used as shops. After passing through the Chhata Chowk one has to pass through Naubat or Nakkar-Khana (Drum House) which was used for playing drums five times a day at propitious hours. Within the Fort, the important buildings include the Diwan-e-Am, the hall where the Emperor held public audience. This is surrounded by open space and a series of marble palaces constructed on the eastern ramparts, by the side of the river. According to the original plan, there were at least six marble structures at irregular intervals, as well as a gate on the side.

The buildings that are well preserved even today are the Mumtaz Mahal, now the Delhi Museum; Rang Mahal, so called because of the coloured decoration in the inner walls; Khas Mahal (private place) consisting of three rooms facing the Diwan-e-Khas and is called Tasbih Khana (chamber of telling beads). The rooms behind it are known as Khawabgah (sleeping chamber); to its south is a long hall known as Tosh Khana (robe chamber). Khuwahgah or Tasbih Khana, Mussamman Burj, Diwan-e-Khas or the hall of private audience, the Hammam to the north of Diwan-e-Khas, Hira Mahal and Shah Burj are some of the other rooms. Architecturally, each structure is in the form of a pavilion with a facade of engrailed arches covered by wide chhajjas and corners embellished with kiosks or chhatris. The surface decoration is mainly seen on pillars and

Top: *Diwan-e-Am*
Middle: *Mumtaz Mahal*
Bottom: *Rang Mahal*

arches, with inlay work of semi-precious stones. Conventional floral motifs are used profusely. The external wall is decorated with features such as balconies or jharokhas and oriel windows, while the terrace is surmounted by gilded cupolas. All this adds to the romance of the legendary fort that once overlooked the River Yamuna. To the west of the Hammam lies a small mosque, called the Moti Masjid (Pearl Mosque) built by Aurangzeb for his personal use. Other important sites in the palace area are two pavilions Sawan and Bhadon (the two principal months of rainy season). In their centre is a pavilion known as Zafar Mahal. As time went by, the miniature city or Shahjahanabad came up around the area chosen by the Emperor for his palace.

Top: *Khas Mahal*
Middle: *Mussamman Burj*
Bottom: *Diwan-e-Khas*

The parameter of this city wall was about 8.8 kilometres and within this area stood rocky ridges, known as the Bhojla and Jugla Paharis. The original walls had a parapet and loopholes for musketry but it is believed, they were hastily built in four months and soon collapsed owing to heavy rain. The city walls had fourteen gateways, fourteen windows and twenty-seven towers, each 10 metres in diameter.

The fourteen gateways of Shahjahanabad included the Kashmere Gate and Mori Gate to the north; Kabuli Gate, Lahori Gate and Ajmeri Gate to the west; Turkman Gate and Delhi Gate to the south; Khairati Gate, Rajghat, Calcutta Gate, Kelaghat, Pathar Gate and Badar

Top: *Hammam, (bathing facility)*
Middle: *Hira Mahal*
Bottom: *Shah Burj*

Rao Gate – all to the east. Among the fourteen windows, the most noticeable is near the Ajmeri Gate. Some of these gateways have been demolished over the years.

The nobles and other affluent people built their separate havelis inside the city walls. A large number of mohallas, katras and kuchas also came up in this area. In Kucha Ghasi Ram lived a great astrologer of the Mughal court who was often consulted by the rulers of Delhi. Ballimaran is named after the ballimars, or oarsmen, who used to row their boats in the central canal of Chandni Chowk. Katra Neel was famous for its indigo sellers.

Top: *Moti Masjid*

Middle: *Sawan and Bhadon pavilions*

Bottom: *Zafar Mahal*

Seth Chunna Mal's haveli

Towards the eastern gate of Katra Neel is the famous haveli of Seth Chunna Mal. This one-hundred-and-twenty-eight-room haveli extends right up to Krishna Market, a well-known wholesale textile market of Chandni Chowk. From its balcony, you can get a magnificent view of Chandni Chowk, in all its splendour, past and present. This haveli was considered a landmark in the city, its occupant attracting the rich and famous of the time. The poet Ghalib has written that, when the rest of the city was plunged in darkness, this beautifully lit haveli stood out and made night look like day.

Seth Chunna Mal was one of the richest men of Shahjahanabad during the British rule. He had a flourishing textile business, dealing in embroidered shawls and exquisite brocades. These goods, the family claims, were supplied to the treasury of the Mughal emperors. Chunna Mal owned several buildings in Chandni Chowk, including Fatehpuri Mosque, which he bought in 1860 for a little over Rs 39,000.

The many factories or karkhanas that sprang up in this area were patronised by the rulers and their nobility.
The city was also meant to provide military security to the limited population that lived within its boundaries.

Adding to Delhi's skyline are other famous monuments.
In fact, during Shah Jahan's reign, his daughter, Roshanara, laid out her grand tomb in 1650. The Jahanara tomb in Nizamuddin was built by her in 1681. It consists of an unroofed small enclosure, walls with lattice marble screens, and a touching inscription on her grave, "Let only the humble grass grow upon my grave. Grass is the best covering for thc poor." One of Shah Jahan's wives, Fatehpuri Begum, built the famous Fatehpuri mosque in 1650 at the western end of Chandni Chowk, also part of Shahjahanabad.

Top: *Jahanara Begum's tomb*
Middle: *Jahanara Begum's grave*
Bottom: *Fatehpuri Mosque*

In front of the eastern gateway of the Jama Masjid lies the Sufi saint Sarmad Sahib's tomb, built in 1659. Close to it is the tomb of his successor, Sayyid Shah Muhammad, also known as Hinga Madani (of Medina). A little to the northeast, on a raised platform, is the grave of Hare Bhare Sahib, built in 1654–1655. Hare Bhare Sahib is believed to have been the spiritual leader of Sarmad Sahib.

Between the Jama Masjid and the Red Fort is the grave of Sheikh Kalimullah Jahanabadi, a pious and learned man of his time. And between the Lahori Gate and the Delhi Gate of Red Fort lies the grave of Sayyid Bhure Shah.

Top: *Hare Bhare Sahib's tomb*

Bottom: *Sufi saint Sarmad Sahib's tomb*

Zinat-ul-Masjid, popularly called Ghata (cloud) Masjid, and almost as striking to look at as the Jama Masjid, is located near the Khairati Ghat, close to the city wall. Built by Alamgir Aurangzeb's daughter, Zinat-un-nisa Begum, it is a major landmark in Daryaganj even today. The mosque is located in a commanding position and consists of a prayer chamber with seven arches and three domes; there are two large minars and a courtyard and a central tank on the river side. Beneath the courtyard are thirteen rooms, terminating on the south and north, with two arched entrances leading up to the court of the mosque.

Top: *Entrance to Hazrat Sheikh Kalimullah Jahanabadi's dargah*

Middle: *Hazrat Sheikh Kalimullah Jahanabadi's dargah*

Bottom: *Sayyid Bhure Shah's dargah*

Zinat-ul-Masjid

It is built of red sandstone, with the exception of the domes, which are banded with black-and-white marble. For many years following the War of Independence of 1857, the mosque was used as a bakery for troops.

Chandni Chowk, or the moonlit square, was built in 1650. It was a large square with a central canal that had cypress trees on either side. It is said that Ali Mardan Khan, Shah Jahan's general and engineer, brought the canal to Chandni Chowk from Tees Hazari Bagh at the request of the Emperor's daughter, Jahanara Begum. From Chandni Chowk the canal was directed to the Red Fort, where Shah Jahan named it Nahar-i-Bahisht, to harmonise it with his overall vision of an earthly paradise. The portion of Chandni Chowk that is visible from the Red Fort, as far as the Dariba, was originally called the Urdu or Military Bazaar.

Important historical buildings have, over the years, been converted for other contemporary usages. For example, at the rear end of the mosque stood the Darul-Baka and the Dar-ush-Shafa which are now occupied by a primary school for

Gurudwara Sisganj and Sunehri Masjid

girls and the Victoria Memorial Hospital for women, respectively.

On the extreme north of the mosque stands the fine building that was once the residence of Begum Samru. Another house of Begum Samru, popularly known as Barud Khana, or Powder Magazine, is situated in the Churiwalan quarter.

Shah Jahan was eager to live up to his image of a great lover of art and architecture. It was he, more than any other emperor, who exerted himself in creating a spectacular display of beauty. That is what makes him one of the most tireless builders in Mughal history.

The Old and the New

Under Shah Jahan's rule, the area around the Jama Masjid was filled with joy and romance. It was rightly known as the cultural meeting place where poetry recitals or mushairas and dance concerts took place. The streets of Shahjahanabad were perfumed and music flowed through its winding lanes. The courtesans who lived here were known to entertain and amuse both the rich and the poor. It was here that poets such as Mirza Ghalib and Meer Taqi Mir sat and penned their masterpieces. No wonder the poet Zauk wrote, *"...kaun jave Dilli ki galiya ko chhodkar"*. He could not resist the heavenly fragrance of a variety of food that emanated from every kucha or basti around the Jama Masjid.

View of the city from the Jama Masjid

The sports and hobbies of the people during those days were varied: kite flying, bird keeping, especially kabutar-bazi on the terrace. Wrestling and cock fights were other favourites.

The Jain Temple in this area dates to the end of the eighteenth century. This exquisite temple has an oblong dome and a rich gilt roof, supported by two rows of small marble columns. The temple has now been extended and gone through many changes. On the west of Dariba was the Phul-ki-Mandi or flower market, up to Kotwali, now known as Gurudwara Sisganj.

It was here that Guru Tegh Bahadur, the ninth Sikh Guru, was martyred on the orders of Emperor Aurangzeb, for espousing the cause of Kashmiri Brahmins. Further ahead lies Dariba or Jauhri Bazaar. It was originally built with arcades of shops. The warehouses and residences of the traders were behind these. Further towards the west, near the Kotwali or police station, was the Roshan-ud-Daula golden mosque, (Sunehri Masjid). This was where the Persian invader Nadir Shah sat while the people of the city were being massacred in March 1739. This brick and plaster mosque was built in 1721 by Roshan-ud-Daula, a courtier during the reign of Muhammad

Top: *Kite flying;* Second Top: *Akhara*
Middle: *Jain Temple*
Bottom: *Gurudwara Sisganj*

Kabutar-bazi on the terrace

Shah. It has three ribbed and spiked domes and eight pinnacles, covered with copper and gilt casings.

The gruesome incident of the massacre is described by an eminent historian of that time: "On the morning of the11th, an order went forth from the Persian emperor for the slaughter of the inhabitants. The result may be imagined; one moment seemed to have sufficed for universal destruction. The Chandni Chowk, the fruit market, the Dariba Bazaar, and the buildings around the Masjid-i-Jama were set fire to and reduced to ashes. The inhabitants, one and all, were slaughtered. Here and there some opposition was offered, but in most places people were butchered unresistingly. The Persians laid violent hands on everything and everybody; cloth, jewels, dishes of gold and silver, were acceptable spoil. But, the Lord be praised, the work of destruction did not extend beyond the above-named parts of the capital. Since the days of Hazrat Sahib-Kiran Amir Timur, who captured Old Delhi and ordered the inhabitants to be massacred, up to the present time, for so many years, the capital had been free from such visitations. The ruin in which its beautiful streets and buildings were now involved was such that the labour of years could alone restore the town to its former state of grandeur.""But to return to the miserable inhabitants. The massacre lasted half the day, when the Persian emperor ordered Haji Faulad Khan, the Kotwal, to proceed through the streets accompanied by a body of Persian Nasakchis, and proclaim an order for the soldiers to desist from carnage. By degrees the violence of the flames subsided, but the bloodshed, the devastation, and the ruin of families were irreparable. For a long time the streets remained strewn with corpses, like a garden strewn with dead flowers and leaves. The town was reduced to ashes. All the regal jewels, property and the contents of the treasury, were seized by the Persian conqueror in the citadel."

"He thus became possessed of treasures to the amount of sixty lakhs of rupees and several thousand ashrafis, a plate of gold, to the value of one crore of rupees, and jewels, many of which were unrivalled in beauty by any in the world, and which were valued at about fifty crores. The Peacock Throne alone, constructed with great pride in the reign of Shah Jahan, had cost one crore of rupees. Elephants, horses and other precious booty, whatever

Portrait of Nadir Shah and Muhammad Shah

pleased the conqueror's eye, more indeed than can be enumerated,became his spoil. In short, the accumulated wealth of so many generations changed masters in a moment."

When Nadir Shah captured the weakening Mughal kingdom in 1739, the first thing on his agenda was to acquire the legendary jewels, the most desirable being the Koh-i-Noor. His attempts drew a frustrating blank, till he was tipped off by a harem informer that the Emperor Mohammed Shah always wore the Koh-i-noor in the pleated folds of his turban.

Nadir Shah chalked out a clever plan. He invited the emperor to a feast at which he proposed an exchange of turbans. Stunned, Mohammad Shah had to agree. And Nadir Shah became the proud owner of this exquisite diamond.

It is such moments that turn the pages of history in an area that is dotted with so many monuments and memories. Among these, in front of the Kotwali, stands a huge fountain named Northbrook, an important landmark in Chandni Chowk.

In the middle of the bazaar, in front of the Kotwali, were the gallows where many leading mutineers met their fate after 1857, including Nawab Abdur Rehman Khan of Jhajjar and Raja Nahar Singh of Ballabgarh. During that time, Darya Ganj, which was the haven of various havelis and gardens, was converted into a cantonment for soldiers.

It was also during the 1857 revolt that the destruction of this historical area reached its high point. More than fifty percent of the interior of the Red Fort was destroyed. The fort, which was designed to provide

View of Coronation Darbar, Delhi

security, began to change its very character. The important palaces for private and public audience, the gardens, the music galleries and the other buildings got converted into military garrisons. The marble-lined canal running down Chandni Chowk was filled up. The trees on both sides were uprooted. The spirit of the bazaars, too, was changing.

A handsome Clock Tower, with four faces and a fine chime of bells, stood in the centre of Chandni Chowk in front of the Town Hall. Unfortunately this most important landmark of Chandni Chowk collapsed after 1950.

A sarai built by Jahanara Begum was replaced by the Town Hall and the gardens behind were redesigned and named Company Bagh. When the railways were introduced in 1860, the entire wall along the northwest was levelled to facilitate the construction of railway tracks. The Jama Masjid was, in fact, confiscated and turned into a stable for the British Army. Ghata Masjid, near Rajghat, was converted into a bakery for troops and the Anglo-Arabic school was converted into a police post.

But after Queen Victoria took over the reins of Delhi during the Delhi Durbar held in Kingsway Camp, the Jama Masjid was once again restored to the local people in 1862. This was also the time that the Fatehpuri Mosque and the Anglo-Arabic School were restored to the residents of the area.Today, in front

Shoppers at Meena Bazaar during the Eid festival

of the eastern or royal gateway of the Jama Masjid are narrow mini-bazaars that overlook another crowded bazaar, known as the Meena Bazaar. Here, a variety of articles ranging from garments and carpets to spare parts, fans, tools and plants are sold. The old buildings have been converted into commercial houses, shops, restaurants and motels. These streets have retained their old-world

Eateries in Chandni Chowk

charm and take the visitor back many centuries. Auto-rickshaws, two-wheelers and cars navigate their way, every single day, through hawkers and vendors who have settled on the pavements of this historical part of the city of Delhi.

No longer can one hear any music nor watch any dance recitals in its meandering lanes. The old city is now a bustling shopping centre, with many small industries. The vegetable and fruit sellers and traders of toys, readymade garments, chappals and other household goods have occupied the large spaces in front of the shops, adding to the colour and local flavour. Perhaps one of the few remnants of the flavour of Shah Jahan's memorable reign is in the form of the famous food that emanated from this area. Nahari, a succulent meat preparation eaten with bread, is popular even today as is evident from the long queue outside the shops that sell it. The meat, although cooked in plenty, is sold out early in the morning. Other mouth-watering offerings from the area include nargisi kofta, badghati badam pasanda, karahi ghosht, kalmi bade, logcha kabab, shahi kabab and so on.

The korma, made exactly the way Shah Jahan liked it, is apparently still available in the vicinity. Little wonder, then, that the Jama Masjid area is known for its enchanting mix of the old and the new.

The Revival

Chaudvi-ka-Chand, an ambitious project undertaken by the Government of India, aims to restore the pristine glory of this area and return Chandni Chowk back to the moonlit square that it was once.

The idea is to give the area a new look by restoring the facades of the old havelis, painting the railings in their original colours, decongesting the traffic and removing ugly signboards. At the time of the launch of this project, cultural programmes were organised, including the reciting of poems, ghazals and mushairas. Special dance performances were held in front of the Fatehpuri Mosque.

Indeed, it was after decades that Chandni Chowk revived some of its lost glory. The busy streets were swept and cleaned and many of the buildings were painted in keeping with the cultural ethos of the area. All the religious buildings in the area around the Jama Masjid, such as the Fatehpuri Mosque, the Digamber Jain Mandir, the Gauri Shankar Mandir, the Central Baptist Church and Gurudwara Sisganj, were also spruced up and decorated. This clean-up drive culminated in a festival that took people back at least a couple of hundred years, when the bazaars were quaint and quiet.

Shopping in Chandni Chowk

Old painting depicting nartaks (dancers)

Following the success of this initiative, another cultural evening was held here and that, too, was very well received. Punjabi pop singers and folk artists came together to perform on the streets of Chandni Chowk, from the Red Fort to Fatehpuri Mosque. There was a Phool Mela that brightened up the entire area; the multi-hued flowers arranged in a variety of shapes such as umbrellas and animals. Camels and elephants, also decorated with flowers, offered joy rides to children.

To facilitate the movement of tourists and to enable them to view the historic city of Shahjahanabad, Delhi Tourism, Delhi Development Authority, the Muncipal Corporation of Delhi, in association with the Indian National Trust for Art and Cultural Heritage (INTACH), Delhi Chapter, and other volunteers have organised heritage walks in Chandni Chowk. The tour which aims to convert Chandni Chowk into a cultural hub, includes a walk which covers Shri Digambar Jain Lal Mandir, Gauri Shankar Temple, the

The Jama Masjid, illuminated

State Bank of India (built in 1806 on Begum Samru's estate), Central Baptist Church (built in 1858), Gurudwara Sisganj, Paranthe Wali Gali, Kinari Bazaar, Naugharana, Katra Kushal Rai, Digambar Jain Naya Mandir, Dharam Pura and Gali Gulian.

It is, indeed, a most interesting walk, allowing one to move in and out of the narrow, winding streets, the mohallas and the havelis of the Nawabs and poets of the time of Emperor Shah Jahan. You can also catch a glimpse of the intricately carved stone pillars, gateways, arches, lattice stone screens and numerous other ornamental pieces of art.

As of now, the past still lives here along with the present, in the most enticing way.

Bhisti or water carrier with a mushak

Mobile water cooler

The Ways

There is always a sense of business humming in the Jama Masjid area and its surroundings. Traders jostle with tourists; devotees with shoppers. And this is how it has always been. The trade most popular around the Jama Masjid during the Mughal period was that of the water carrier (bhisti). During the days of the Mughal kings, the job of providing water to the Muslims who used to visit the mosque for prayer was carried out by these bhistis, purely on philanthropic terms and no money was charged. This tradition continues even today and many bhistis do not ask for any money for supplying water, though they do accept it when offered to them.

In Delhi, around the Jama Masjid, they carry their water bags (mushaks) that were originally made from camel hide, but today there are very few of them. These bags are excellent as water can be kept cold for at least six hours in them without imbibing any odour. These mushaks are durable and can last for many years without wear and tear. They are now replaced with a combination of canvas tarpaulin and leather. This option is much cheaper but does not keep the water cold for long. Also the water loses its original refreshing aroma. Nevertheless, they are most sought after in the summer months in the Jama Masjid area. Nowadays, ice is also put in the mushak. The work of these bhistis is greatly affected these days with modern day competition – portable water coolers, soft drink and nimbu pani vendors.

Besides the bhistis of the Jama Masjid, you also come across a few people who run astabals (stables). One such person, who resides in the Jama Masjid Madarasa Hussain Baksh Gali, still maintains a stable that he dates to the time of Shah Jahan. He claims that his ancestors reared horses for Mughal soldiers as well as for sportsmen and owned many of the stables till the time of the War of Independence in 1857. After that most of the stables were either sold or forcibly taken away by the British. Another stable exists in the Jama Masjid area, right where the tonga stand is located.

Tum tums and havadars, open carriages with convertible roofs, can still be seen in this vicinity. These were used mainly by the nobles and the members of the family of the Emperor. These carriages were driven by horses, but were replaced by the tonga, which, in turn, is being replaced by the popular, omnipresent cycle rickshaw. The other kind of traditional carriage seen in this area was the doli, which was used to carry brides

Top: *Tonga carrying tourists*
Second Top: *Cycle rickshaw*
Second Bottom: *Tourist bus*
Bottom: *Auto rickshaw*

to their grooms' houses. The British had introduced the tram car, with a terminal at the Jama Masjid. It had a circular route, all along Old Delhi, passing through Chandni Chowk. This no longer exists.

Cars and auto rickshaws are slowly taking over in a place that was known for its astonishing variety of transport. These included the traditional palanquins, bullock-carts or recklas and the more modern horse-drawn conveyances such as phaetons or buggies, the dhamney, an enclosed carriage and the single bullock-drawn ekka.

This is the inevitable effect of modernisation in a tranquil area where time was meant to stand still. Where the mosque stands, a tribute to its creator and as a silent witness of changing times and generations. Yet, somehow, even today, when you climb those red sandstone steps and look up at the Jama Masjid, just for that one short moment, you feel transported in time. You see before you a great Emperor, a grand plan, a grandiose vision. And all this comes together in perfect harmony in the splendour that is the Jama Masjid.

Top: *Covered palanquin*

Second Top: *Open palanquin pulled by a bullock*

Second Bottom: *Havadar (a tonga with a convertible roof)*

Bottom: *Rath (a covered vehicle for ladies of the first rank)*

The Renewal

Eid is a word that has actually been derived from the Arabic 'Oud' (عود) which means repetition. Eid-ul-Fitr is a reward from God for all those who have gone through Ramzan, the month of fasting preceding the festival. Fasting is a sure test of devotion, especially in the sweltering heat of summer when nothing is eaten or a drop of water drunk from early dawn to dusk and a person experiences sharp pangs of hunger, thirst, fatigue and weakness. Abstaining not only from food and water but also from all the mundane evils of routine life makes a person thoroughly disciplined, inculcating in him the qualities of endurance, compassion for the destitute and complete submission to Allah the great. Fasting also induces in an individual the habit to refrain from negative thinking, ill conceived and hastily executed initiatives and anything that might harm others. Abstinence accompanied by rigorous fasting purifies a person.

Hazrat Prophet Mohammad (peace be upon him) celebrated his first Eid on March 27, 624 A.D. with the orphans and destitute, who actually were his dear and near ones, on the outskirts of Medina. Prior to the advent of Eid in Medina there was no other occasion to celebrate cumulatively like this. In the course of time, Eid-ul-Fitr became the greatest occasion

Offering Eid prayers at the Jama Masjid

of this community. Before going to t he prayers of Eid-ul-Fitr, it is mandatory that every prosperous Muslim must donate some money to all the underprivileged, so that they too can participate in the festivity.

The night before Eid is known as 'Shab-e-Qadar' (night of praying). Early in the morning the faithfuls, after bathing, eat their breakfast, which is usually something sweet, such as sewaiyan (vermicelli), sheer khurma or sheerni. Doing it is a part of Sunnah (an activity done by the Hazrat Prophet Mohammad), that is why this Eid is also known as Meethi Eid (Sweet Eid). The holy Prophet Mohammad used to eat dates on this occasion.

Eid-ul-Fitr was celebrated with fervour and intensity during the time of Shah Jahan. The excitement and enthusiasm percolated down to all. Even today, Eid is celebrated in Delhi with an inimitable style and aura of its own.

Ibn-e-Batuta, a famous Arab chronicler, refers to this festival in his travelogue, *Saffarname-e-ibn-e-Batuta*. He writes: "If one desires to relish the carnival joys of Eid, one must visit the place where the heart of India lies – Delhi, a place where people feel the pulse of absolute bliss."

The Jama Masjid on the night before Eid

Ramzan is the ninth month of the Muslim year. It is a period of great importance in Islamic practice for it is believed that on the first night of Ramzan, all rebellious jinns or devils are shackled, the gates of hell are closed and the doors of heaven are thrown open. A heralder then calls out each night: "You, who want to do good, come forward and you, who want to do evil, stop." In accordance with the lunar calendar, Ramzan may occur in extremes of cold and heat or in seasons when the days may be either very long or very short. The month of Ramzan begins with the sighting of the waxing moon and concludes when the moon is first seen in the next month, Shawwal. If the moon cannot be sighted, it ends with the completion of thirty fasts. It is during Ramzan that the Jama Masjid area offers its most delectable treasures. Shops in the Jama Masjid area offer delicacies such as the matchless bakar khani, shahi tukra and rabri, a thickened and sweetened milk. Another dish enjoyed by all is biryani. The rice is cooked with chicken or mutton with a mild combination of spice and saffron. Large carts full of biryani can be seen in the area in the late evening when fasts are broken.

An enclosure reserved for women

Muslim women offering Namaz

Brassware stall during Eid festival

Eid enthusiasm around the Jama Masjid area exceeds and outlasts all other places in the city. During Eid, cobblers, hair-dressers, milkmen, grocers, bangle sellers, hosiery sellers and the halwais around the Jama Masjid are in great demand. On Eid a plethora of festivities take place here. The festive mood is

Embracing and greeting each other with "Eid Mubarak"

infectious. Burqa-clad women are seen with their little ones, buying new clothes, shoes, toys and fire-crackers. Girls dressed in their best clothes gather around the bangle sellers. The young and old both wear traditional embroidered topis.

Muslims and non-Muslims embrace and greet each other with "Eid Mubarak." The entire lawn of Jama Masjid, its steps and even the road outside the mosque, are filled with thousands of devotees.

Throughout the nights, the streets around Jama Masjid are illuminated with dazzling lights. It is in this area that the hearts of Muslims pulsate. You can see them crowding the streets, enjoying iftaar. Groups of people gather along the roadside, relishing their glass of sherbet, or mango and milk with a spoonful of malai. Although the meat shops are open throughout the day, the real rush is seen when the handis are unsealed in the evening. In the month of Ramzan, when the faithful break their fasts after sunset, the handiwalas open after the evening prayers and traditional items such as sewaiyan, palm dates and fruits are sold in great quantities.

Halwai's shop

Iftaar is the most cherished time during the thirty days of Ramzan. It is an occasion for reunion and reconciliation, fasting and feasting. It is this moment at sunset that is considered a time of bliss. Iftaar evenings are eagerly awaited. For, they spell camaraderie and assure a good time for all. Each night, the area around the Jama Masjid glitters with dazzling lights and throbs with life. During Iftaar, temporary and rudimentary eating stalls multiply on the roadside, with wooden chairs and tables laid with cheap plastic sheets, offering tantalising food. The lights that illuminate the grand Jama Masjid make the ambience even more special. The mosque and its surrounding bylanes are the places to

Sewaiyan are in great demand during the Eid festival

visit during this festive period.

The area comes alive soon after the zuhar namaz (afternoon prayer), with eateries opening up at every conceivable nook and corner. The shops are illuminated with colourful lights. Film music gives way to Quranic cassettes and na'ats (hymns in praise of Prophet Muhammad).

Vendor's pushcarts and roadside squatters around the Jama Masjid further contribute to the ambience. Shops with neatly stacked sweets bustle with activity. And, as you walk past the Masjid, inside one can see a sea of whitecapped heads rising and bowing in a synchronised manner. This is prayer time. There is an overall air of sobriety when so many

During Iftaar temporary stalls come up in the Jama Masjid area

gather to offer their collective prayers. Every evening, during the namaz, a sense of calm descends upon the otherwise traffic-congested areas. Indeed, there is no better place to be at during this time than the Jama Masjid, with its aura of grandeur and majesty. And its environs add to the joyousness of the moment.

Another festive occasion, equally important and auspicious, is the Eid Milad-un-Nabi, the birthday of Holy Prophet Hazarat Muhammad (peace be upon him). This, too, is celebrated throughout the country, but with more gaiety around the Jama Masjid as night-long prayers are held here.

The Holy Prophet Hazrat Muhammad was born in Mecca on the 12th day of the month of Rabiul' Awwal in the year 570 A.D. (approximately) and was appointed

Panoramic view of the Jama Masjid

a prophet of Islam in the year 610 A.D. (approximately). Maulanas and Islamic scholars highlight the principles of Islam. A colourful procession, passing through old Delhi, culminates at the Jama Masjid. Tableaux, horses, camels and elephants all form part of this procession.

The mosque is decorated with lights and colourful gates, in consonance with the spirit of the festivities. Food is distributed among the poor for these two days.

Eid-ul-Ada or Eid-ul-Zuha (Bakr-Eid) is one of the grandest Muslim festival. It means an Eid of sacrifice. The word Eid, derived from the Arabic 'Iwd', means 'festival'. Zuha comes from 'Uzhaiyya', which translates to sacrifice. On this day, congregational prayers are offered along with qurbani (sacrifice) and goods offered to others. Eid-ul-Zuha is a lesson in sacrifice, exhorting the believers that they have to be prepared for self sacrifice, without which the responsibilities of life cannot be fulfilled.

The aim of sacrifice, like all other fundamentals of Islam, is to imbibe piety and self righteousness. It also promotes the spirit of sacrifice for a right cause. Sacrifice during the days of Eid-ul-Adha is waajib (compulsory) for all Muslims. This festival of sacrifice is celebrated two months and ten days after Eid-ul-Fitr.

There is an interesting story about the celebration. Once, the Hazrat Ibrahim

Faithful offering namaz

was ordered by Allah in a dream to sacrifice his dearest thing. To Ibrahim his son was his dearest thing. Ibrahim, having implicit faith in God, decided to offer the sacrifice and brought his son on the altar of Allah. He sought the permission of the members of the family and blindfolded himself so that at the time of sacrifice his love for his son may not deter him from the act. He struck with his sword, but when he removed the fold from his eyes, to his great pleasure and surprise, he found that he had sacrificed a ram instead of his son.

Since then, for Bakri-Eid, every Muslim family is required to sacrifice a healthy animal and distribute two-third of the meat among the poor.

Shoppers throng the markets during the festive season

The sacrifice of a ram or goat also symbolises that man's position in the creation is far higher than any beast, and any sacrifice, however great, is a small thing for the sake of religion and Allah.

On Bakri-Eid, Muslims go to the mosques in the morning to offer prayers to Allah and then sacrifice the animal at home.

Celebrations on the first day include 'Do Wakat Namaz', which can be performed any time from sunrise to just after noon. The prayers during this festival are considered more rewarding than other daily or weekly offerings. Prophet Muhammad had decreed that the entire community celebrates Eid for three days to facilitate participation.

Prayer meetings and Eid Milans are part of the festivities. People visit friends and relatives wearing new clothes and jewellery. Children are given idi or gifts and money. In the Indian sub-continent sweets are exchanged. Vermicelli or sewaiyan, a traditional sweet, is prepared specially for this festival.

It is said that during the period of ignorance, people of Medina had fixed two days for merry-making and

entertainment, which were replaced later by Eid-ul-Fitr and Eid-ul-Adha after Prophet Muhammad migrated from Mecca to Medina. The Jama Masjid is the place to visit during this time of prayer. On this day, the Imam of Jama Masjid delivers the sermons to the faithful who assemble here for Eid prayers.

In earlier times, on Fridays, the khutbah was read, which was a prayer for the reigning emperor. It recounted his titles, possibly including his predecessors', but now only a sermon follows. The Imam preaches from the middle steps of the pulpit. On occasions the azan, or call to prayer, is made by muezzins who stand in colonnades around the court, facing towards Mecca, their hands raised on either side of the head. They declare, loud and clear: "Allah is great. I bear witness that Allah is God, Muhammad is the prophet of Allah, haste to prayer, haste to salvation in the morning only, here added prayer is better than sleep, Allah is great, Allah is the only God."

Thousands of devotees come to the Jama Masjid during Eid. It is believed that if anybody wishes to relish the joys of Eid they should only come here, to the magnificent Jama Masjid, for this is where the heart of India throbs.

Devotees offering prayers at the Jama Masjid

Muharram is observed with solemnity. It is a period of mourning for the Shia devotees. For, it marks the death of Hazarat Imam Hussain, the grandson of Prophet Muhammad and the son of Ali and Fatima, in a seventh century battle for leadership of the Islamic world.

It is believed that Hussain confronted Yazid of the Umayyad dynasty on the tenth day of the Islamic holy month of Muharram. Many members of his family were killed on this fateful day by Muawiahi (Banu Ummayya), the ruler of Syria.

On this day every year, the tazia procession of Shias marking Ashoura, the treacherous and brutal death of Hussain, is led through the lanes surrounding the Jama Masjid, right up to a karbala in New Delhi. Here, the tazia is buried with tears.

Tears and joy; festivals and merrymaking; prayer and devotion...the Jama Masjid has been spectator to it all. The monument tells its story; its stones speak as the Masjid fervently calls out to the soul.

Facing page: *Muharram procession passing through the streets of the Jama Masjid area*

Left: *Muharram procession with the tazia*

Acknowledgements

I am grateful to the Archaeological Survey of India (ASI), particularly Mrs Achala Moulik, its then Director General, for giving me permission to use photographs and drawings from the ASI.

I am also grateful to Mr JP Joshi and Mr MC Joshi Ex-Directors General, ASI, who inspired me to write this book. I am indebted to my senior colleagues, Mr BM Pandey, Mr RC Aggarwal and Mr RC Sharma, and others in the ASI, for their encouragement and support.

This book has involved intensive research for which I have referred to various books on architecture, and selected writings of Dr Firoz Bakht Ahmed.

Care has been taken to interpret important historical events in a fair manner and ensure the accuracy of dates and facts. The endeavour throughout Call of the Soul has been to present the Jama Masjid in all its magnificence. There is no intention of hurting the sentiments of any individual, group or community, and if that should appear inadvertently, I would like to reiterate that this is not my intent. This book is, quite simply, a tribute to this special monument.

NL Batra

Artist at work

Bibliography

A. Cunningham : Archaeological Survey of India, Reports

Bernier, Francois : Travels in the Mogul Empire, 1656-1688

Brown, Percy : Indian Architecture (Islamic period)

Cole, H.H. : The Architecture of Ancient Delhi

Duncan, E.A. : Keen's Handbook for Visitors to Delhi

Fanshwe, H.C. : Shahjahan's Delhi – Past and Present

Fergusson, I. : History of Indian Architecture

Flatcher, Banistor : A History of Architecture

Havell, E.B. : Indian Architecture

Nath, R. : History of Sultanate Architecture

Mc Kay, R.B. : Building Construction, Vol. I, II, III

Page, J.B. : A Historical Memoir of the Qutb

Sanderson, Gorden : List of Muhammadan and Hindu monuments

Sayyid Ahmed Khan : Asar-us-Sanadid (Urdu) Delhi Monuments

Sharma, Y.D. : Delhi and its Neighbourhood

Sir John Marshal : Archaeological Survey of India, Annual Reports

Spear, T.G.P. : Delhi: Its Monuments and History, Oxford University Press, 1943

Zaffar Hasan : Monuments of Delhi, Lasting Splendour of the Great Mughals and Others (Reprint, New Delhi, 1997)

Maulana Wahiduddin Khan : 'Islam As it is', Islamic centre publisher, Nizzamuddin, New Delhi

Pir Syed Ahmad Sarmadi : Tazakara (discussion) Hazarat Sarmad Shahid (in Urdu) Kutab Khana Sarmadi, Jama Masjid, Delhi

Glossary

Taking into account the peculiarities of a language and the concept of the 'intranslatable' word, the meanings given here refer to the contextural framework of the book and merely help in understanding the text.

[A]

Allah	the Almighty God
Alcove	vaulted recess in wall
Arabesque	decoration with fanciful intertwining of ornamental elements
Arcade	range of arches supported on piers or columns
Arcuate	arched

[B]

Badam pasanda	meat preparation with a mixture of almond and spicy gravy
Balcony	outside balustrade platform
Baluster	balustrade, a small pillar or column supporting a handrail
Bakar khani	delicacy of meat preparation
Bas-relief	carving of low projection
Basti	colony
Bastion	projecting part of a fortification
Batter	slope, rake
Battlements	indented parapet, kanjur
Bay	division or compartment; between pillars, a chauki
Bazaar	market
Beam	lintel, long piece of stone or wood supported at each end
Biryani	rice pullav mixed with vegetables or cooked chicken or meat
Boss	ornamental projection in the form of a large knob
Bracket	projecting ornament or support
Brahmins	caste in Hindus
Bulbous	shaped like a bulb, nearly spherical
Burj	tower
Burqa	dress women put on to cover themselves

[C]

Centring	temporary construction on which the stones of the arch are mounted
Chajja	overhanging cornice, eave
Chhatri	kiosks, or small pavilions, acting as turrets on the roof
Cloisters	arched bay, liwan
Core	inner construction of a wall or other architectural feature
Cornice	projection
Corridor	passage in a building
Cramp	metal bar for holding masonry
Crenellated	furnished with battlements or loopholes
Cupola	spherical roof
Cusp	cusped, projecting point between small arcs of an archway

[D]

Dargah	in India designation of a Mohammadan shrine or tomb
Diaper	small floral pattern repeated continuously over a wall surface
Diwan-e-Am	hall of public audience in a Mohammadan palace
Diwan-e-Khas	hall of private audience in a Mohammadan palace
Double dome	composed of an inner and outer shell of masonry
Do Waqat-Namaz	two times prayer
Drum or collar	circular wall on which the dome rests
Durbar	Indian court or levee

[E]

Eid-ul-Fitr	month of fasting (a festival), a reward from God for those who have gone through Ramzan
Eid-ul-Uzah	festival of sacrifice (Bakr-Eid)
Engrailed	foliated, cusped; an arch having an arch within its curves
Extrados	upper or outer curve in arch construction

[F]

Facade	front view or elevation
Faluda	kind of drink, its main ingredient prepared from parched, ground wheat
Filigree	fine ornamental work, delicate tracery
Finial	finishing portion of a pinnacle
Flange	projecting flat rim, collar or rib
Fluting	vertical channeling on the shaft of a column
Frieze	upper border: middle division of entablature

[G]

Gali	small street or lane
Ghazi	the conqueror
Ghosht	meat (mutton)
Guldasta	small turret-like termination, pinnacle
Gumbad	local name (Delhi), for a dome, or domed tomb
Gumbaz	dome

[H]

Halwais	sweet sellers
Hammam	Turkish bath
Haveli	huge residential house with central courtyard
Huzrah	tomb-chamber in a Mohammadan tomb
or Estanah	
Hybrid	mixture of elements of Hindu and Muslim architecture

[I]

Ibadat Khana	prayer hall
Imam-ul-Sultan	Shahi Imam, appointed by the emperor
Impost	member on which the arch immediately rests
Intrados	inside surface of an arch

[J]

Jali	any lattice or perforated pattern
Jamb	sides of the openings of doors and windows
Jami Masjid	congregational mosque
Jauhri Bazaar	market where silver, gold and diamonds are traded

[K]

Kanjura	stepped battlement, merlon
Kabutar-bazi	a sport or hobby of keeping pigeons
Kalmi bade	a unique combination of mutton shaped in different forms
Kankar lime	a granular limestone dug from fields
Khakan	emperor
Khutbah	address or sermon delivered by the Imam on the occasion of Eid or Friday prayer
Kinari Bazaar	brocade bazaar
Kiosk	chattri, small pavilion, generally on parapet or roof
Korma	recipe transformed into a royal treat
Kotwal	police station house officer
Kotwali	police post
Kutcha	residential complex, mohallas

[L]

Lattice	marble screens, a jali work in marble
Liwan	pillared cloisters of a mosque
Logcha kabab	mixture of mutton/chicken and spices shaped into cylindrical cutlets

[M]

Machicolation	parapet of fortress with openings for dropping missiles
Madrassa	school, college
Mahal	palace
Malai	layer of thickened milk

Mansebdars	status given to the nobles according to their worth
Mazar	dargah, pavilion with graves
Minarah	call to prayer
Maqbarah	mortuary chamber of a Mohammadan tomb
Maqsura	screen or arched facade of a mosque
Masjid	mosque, or 'place of prostration'
Mausoleum	large tomb building
Mihrab	niche or arched recess in the western wall of an Indian mosque towards which worshippers turn for prayer
Mimbar	pulpit in mosque
Minar	minaret, slender turret of a mosque from which the muezzin gives the call to prayer
Moat	deep wide ditch surrounding a fort
Mohallas	residential complex, kutcha
Mortar	mixture of lime, sand, and water for joining stones or bricks
Moulding	contour given to projecting members
Moulvis	teacher of Islamic scriptures
Muezzin	person who calls the faithful for prayer
Mujahid	warrior in the cause of God
Mukkabir	person who assists the Imam by announcing the time during which the various motions in the prayer are regulated
Musketeers	soldiers who used guns with long barrels
Musketry	loopholes in the parapet wall used for firing from long barrel guns
Muskets	gun with a long barrel used in the past
Mussamon Burj	solid or strong bastion
Mutakka	stepped parapet, kanjura
Muzinah	minar from where the faithful are summoned

[N]

Nahari	succulent meat preparation
Nahar-i-Bahisht	canal of paradise
Naqqar Khana	Drum House, arched structure to announce arrival by beat of drum
Nargasi kofta	recipe of mutton shaped into mini balls in gravy
Nasakchis	shooters
Naubat Khana	same as Naqqar Khana
Naugharana	nine sectors
Nave	central or main compartment of a building
Naya Mandir	new temple
Niche	recess in wall for the reception of a stature or ornament
Nimbu pani	lemon water
Noble	person belonging to high social rank

[O]

Omrahs (Umrah)	plural of Arabic, Amir (wealthy)
Opus sectile	marble intarsia (inlay) of various colours
Oriel	projecting window

[P]

Palkey	palanquin
Panel	sunken compartment in a wall
Parapet	upper portion of a wall, above the roof
Pavilion	chavada, chabutra
Pendentive	triangular surface by which a dome is supported on a square compartment
Phase of Transition	structural system by which a square hall alters its shape above in order to accommodate the circular base of a dome
Phool Mela	flower festival
Pilaster	square pillar projecting from a wall
Pike men	soldiers with pike (a long sharp stick)
Pinnacle	guldasta, small turret-like termination

Plan — representation of a building showing the general distribution of its parts in horizontal section
Plinth (Piha) — lower portion, or base, of a building or column
Pulpit — mimber or mimbras

[Q]

Qibla — direction for prayer
Qila — fort
Quwwat-ul-Islam — might of Islam

[R]

Rabri — thickened milk
Rang Mahal — painted palace, one of the most sumptuous pavilions in a palace-fortress
Rauza — large and important Mohammadan tomb
Reliquary — receptacle for relics
Rib — projecting band on a ceiling or vault

[S]

Sahn — open courtyard of a mosque
Sarai — caravan sarai, halting place
Seraglio — walled palace
Sewaiyan — sweet vermicelli
Shaft — portion of a column between base and capital
Shahi kabab — unique combination of different ingredients shaped into cylindrical cutlets
Shahi tukra — unique delicacy
Sharbat — sweet drink
Sheer kurma or Sheerni — sweetened vermicelli in thickened milk
Soffit — underside of any architectural member
Sonehri — golden
Spandrel — triangular space between the curve of an arch and the square enclosing it
Squinch arch — arches placed diagonally at angles in the interiors of domes
Sultan — emperor
Suna — religious practice

[T]

Taikhana — basement chamber
Tantpur — name of a place in Rajasthan
Tracery — ornamental perforated pattern
Transept — cross or transverse compartments of a building
Tum-tum — open carriage with convertible roof
Turrets — small towers

[V]

Vault — arched covering over any space
Veneer stones — facing stones
Voussoir — wedge-shaped block forming a true arch

[Y]

Ya-Hadi — address to the God or Guide for the right path

[Z]

Zafar Mahal — palace of Emperor Bahadur Shah Zafar

Index